The Crypto Book

*How to Invest Safely in Bitcoin and
Other Cryptocurrencies*

SIAM KIDD

T0054383

JOHN
MURRAY
LEARNING

First published in Great Britain by John Murray Learning in 2018
An imprint of John Murray Press
A division of Hodder & Stoughton Ltd,
An Hachette UK company

This paperback edition published in 2022

5

A CIP catalogue record for this title is available from the British Library

Paperback ISBN 978 1 473 69332 6
Trade Paperback ISBN 978 1 473 69331 9
eBook ISBN 978 1 473 69333 3
Audio ISBN 978 1 473 69334 0

Typeset by KnowledgeWorks Global Ltd.

Printed and bound in Great Britain by Clays Ltd, Elcograf S.p.A.

John Murray Press policy is to use papers that are natural, renewable and recyclable
products and made from wood grown in sustainable forests. The logging and
manufacturing processes are expected to conform to the environmental regulations of
the country of origin.

John Murray Press
Carmelite House
50 Victoria Embankment
London EC4Y 0DZ

www.johnmurraypress.co.uk

**Also available
as an ebook**

Contents

About this book

The aim of this book is to turn you from a typical crypto noob (newbie) into a competent crypto investor/speculator, with a basic investment framework to lean on. I'll tell you what you *actually* need to know in order to step into this murky world and profit from it.

I've designed this book to be as easy to read as possible. You're not going to be learning the inner workings of cryptographic laws and blockchain architecture because it isn't necessary. Instead, you'll find lots of bite-sized chapters that you can read quickly and refer back to if you ever have a question in the future.

I'd also like to invite you to join my community of switched-on crypto investors. I have the world's best crypto investing course for beginners, according to many of my students. The course's private Facebook group is a hive of activity and many students have made huge profits from the course and my crypto alerts. During 2017 my crypto alerts made the community over £3 million in combined profits. It's a fantastic group of positive people playing with cryptos and I really want to see this community grow.

Just visit www.TheRealisticTrader.com to find out more.

I
Why I've written this guide

Cryptocurrency: A digital currency in which encryption techniques are used to regulate the generation of units of currency and verify the transfer of funds, operating independently of a central bank.

Oxford English Dictionary online

It doesn't matter what level you're at right now. You may be clueless about cryptos but intrigued by what you've heard, or you may have bought a few mainstream cryptos like Bitcoin, Ether or Litecoin. You may even be storing them on an exchange (which, as you'll find out later, is asking for trouble).

If this sounds like you, you're in the right place. I will equip you with a finely tuned crypto BS detector and all the necessary information you need to decide whether this crazy market is the right fit for you – and vice versa.

But before we begin, let's go back in time a bit …

Back in 2010 I took the plunge and quit my dream job. Ever since I was a kid I'd always wanted to be a Royal Air Force pilot and I dedicated every waking moment of my childhood to becoming one. After many hard years of chasing my dream and being called 'space cadet' at school, it all finally paid off when I became an officer at the age of 18 and got my 'wings' a few years later. It was great. I was being paid to fly, travel the world, and play with some pretty cool toys. I'll never forget the first time I flew with night-vision goggles; it was just surreal.

I've had some of the best memories of my life in the Air Force, but I had to escape. I had to get out of that militarized rat race. Yes, many perks came with the job but, in reality, 90 per cent of it was a mind-numbing chore of waking up early, shaving every day, being told what to do, spending five hours or more planning maps and logistics for an hour of flying, and the extra duties you had to do as an officer.

Also, I was becoming increasingly aware of a condition known in the Air Force as AIDS: Aircraft Induced Divorce Syndrome. Pretty much every pilot I knew above the age of 40 was divorced or having a midlife crisis and many also had money troubles. It was a vortex that I thoroughly wanted to avoid.

My trading, which I started when I was 18, was beginning to come good. Well, I say good: the truth was more that I was no longer burning money at an alarming rate. For the first few years I was the worst trader on the planet; I lost £50 k in my first year and then continued to burn £2,000 per month – *every* month – for a solid four years. It was painful. I pretty much had a gambling problem and my stubbornly thick brain couldn't get the hang of it all! With hindsight, my ego was hindering my progress. The idiot youth inside me was thinking, 'If I can fly planes in the military, surely everything else in life is easy.' How wrong I was!

After six years I actually started to become consistently profitable, but it definitely *wasn't* due to being a whizz kid on the markets. I just had six years of stepping on landmines under my belt. Through trial and error, I learned what *not* to do.

So around late 2009 I had a convergence of exit signals. My trading was improving and I began to dislike my job. Wealth generation became my new obsession and I quickly realized that I'd never hit the monthly income goal I had set myself in the military. To top it all off, I scared myself witless on a couple of flights because I was just thinking about the trades I had running instead of flying the aircraft. My focus definitely wasn't on flying. I did less prep, put in less effort and started to fail some rather elementary tests. It was a recipe for eventual disaster.

I had to leave.

My job became totally incongruent with my new life goals. And the first one was to sort myself out financially and hit my £20,000 per month take-home target. After a Christmas of deliberation, in early 2010 I executed the '7 clicks to freedom'. There is a personnel system in the Air Force where you can effectively hit the Career Nuke Button and bang out of the mob by sacrificing a monumental chunk of your pension and other perks.

I've learned a lot since leaving the Air Force. From 2010 to 2014 I was an utter failure. My first three businesses flopped, I ran up a £130 k debt and I was forced to borrow £10 k from my parents to prevent personal bankruptcy. The road to success is never as straightforward as in the movies. I now know that success is like a Space X rocket launch: years of preparation and failure on the ground and then – boom. The success bit happens in a couple of minutes!

Fast-forward to today. It's late 2017, and I'm in Vegas tapping away at the keyboard, resisting the pull of the 'strip'. I now own seven profitable businesses and have fingers in a few other companies. I've hit many of my financial targets, including my original monthly income goal. I've got my dream car (I like my toys), live in a house I thought it would take 20 years to achieve, and I've just finished speaking to a huge audience about cryptocurrencies at the US Money Show.

And in 2015 I achieved a personal record on the markets by making just over £420 k in 30 minutes at home while I sat in my underwear during the Black Monday Crash.

So what have I learned?

1 **When it comes to investing, often the thing you really don't want to do is the thing you really need to do.**

   If wealth generation were easy, everyone would be rich, right? I see too many people being miserable about their lives who aren't willing to get up and do something about it. I once met a guy in the USA who moaned that where he lived was always cold. I told him he wasn't a tree! All he needed to do was pack his stuff into a van and move south. In my case, leaving the dream job I dedicated most of my life to was a really tough pill to take. And for four hard years I thoroughly regretted it.

Joining the Air Force was the best thing I've ever done, but leaving it was the second-best. So if you, too, are in a position that isn't in line with what you want to do … PIVOT!

2 **Whenever you are presented with a good opportunity, you have to reach out, grab it and dominate it.** Some opportunities will work out, some won't. It's all about the risk-to-reward ratio. When the potential reward is considerable, you need only a small win rate. If I ever come across an opportunity with a 1:10 risk-to-reward ratio (10R), I'll take it, regardless of my opinions. For example, if something presents itself where I risk £1, but it has the potential to reward me with £10, I'll be all over it. Every now and then, one of those opportunities morphs into a 100R outcome. Wealth generation is just a numbers game, and you only need one or two big hits to set yourself up. That's why you need to allocate a small portion of your capital (risk capital) that is constantly swinging for the fences. In this book's case, cryptocurrencies are anything from a 10 to a 1000R play …

3 **You need to know how to avoid the scammers out there.** We saw it during the tech bubble in the early 2000s, and we're seeing it again now. A whole bunch of amateurs are popping out of nowhere pretending to be Bitcoin or crypto investing experts, but 99 per cent of the time they're far from it. They're spreading misleading and incorrect information that will end up biting them — and you. Yes, you can spend hours on YouTube and Google learning everything you can about cryptos, but

knowing the theory won't make you a good investor. Just like those new millionaires who go out and buy themselves a Ferrari and imagine they can drive like Lewis Hamilton, the inevitable outcome is pain. Luckily for you, scammers are easy to spot. Long story short, knowing about cryptos and becoming a competent investor are two completely different skills.

I've written this book to share everything I've learned about the world of crypto investing, so that you, too, can profit from this radical world of virtual currency trading.

2
The crucial difference between money and currency

'Money isn't everything, but it's right up there with oxygen!'

Zig Ziglar

It may seem a bit odd starting the first main chapter of the book on a topic you think you know well, but you are mistaken. I speak to thousands of people across the globe every year and, whether it's on stage or in conversation, I use the opportunity to probe people's understanding of money. Guess what? It's not as good as it should be.

It's ironic, seeing as we all spend our blood, sweat, tears, talent and time trying to earn it. And most of us are still completely oblivious to what it really is, how it flows, how it's created, and, more importantly, how to get it, keep it and multiply it. Money isn't everything, but it's the best stepping stone to achieving the real goal of health, wealth and happiness. And wealth in this context is freedom – freedom to do whatever you want, whenever you want, with whomever you want.

You'll find that as your financial wealth ascends, your views on money also change. Once you get to financial independence and the stresses and strains of financial heartache pass, it's as if a huge weight has been lifted off your shoulders and you suddenly have a clearer lens to look through. Money no longer holds a compelling grip over your life and psyche and you can think clearly about bigger things. Oh, and you'll probably start spending money trying to get back the health you sacrificed in the pursuit of money in the first place.

I remember reading self-help books back when I was stone broke in 2010, so I'm aware that this may all sound pretentious. I read amazing teachings from billionaires and titans of industry with their philanthropic views. But, when you're struggling to feed your family and pet dog and cat, money is literally the only thing you care about.

To properly master money, first you need to understand it. You need to know the game you're playing. And if you don't know the rules of the game, you're going to get slaughtered, just like 99.99 per cent of the population who are destined to remain on the financial merry-go-round. It's not your fault if you're born into poverty, but, if you die in poverty, that is your fault. All it takes is a little bit of effort to learn the game and you'll do wonders for yourself.

This is even more important in the realm of cryptos. If you don't *precisely* understand money, you'll never fully grasp cryptos and the sheer importance of what they will do to the world and how to capitalize on them. Probably the most important phrase of this book to remember is this:

> **Cryptos are the EVOLUTION of currency and blockchain is the REVOLUTION of trust.**

Some people say that this is a money revolution, but it's not. It's much bigger than that. The transition into cryptos is as big as the transition from bartering to coined money in 700 BCE.

What is money?

Money is essentially three things:

- A unit of measure
- A medium of exchange
- A store of wealth.

It's not often I get sucked down into the weeds of definitions, but being pedantic in your knowledge of money will help you see through a lot of nonsense in the future relating to what banks, governments and cryptos are doing. Breaking down the definition even further, there are seven things money *has to be*:

1 **A unit of measure**, so you can accurately gauge how much something is worth.

2 **A medium of exchange**, so you can transact with someone else efficiently without bartering your own goods for other goods. Bartering is terribly inefficient due to the necessity of requiring the right thing for the right person at the right time. For example, if you have chickens and you need milk from the farmer, you can get it only if the farmer wants chickens as a means of payment. If not, no milk for you.

3 **Fungible**, so your unit of money can be recognized by other people in other places. That way, we can all agree that the money we both hold is the same.

4 **Divisible**, so you can break it into smaller bits to buy cheaper things.

5 **Durable**, so it can withstand different climates, temperatures and transportation. This is why food can never be money.

6 **Portable**, so you can transport large amounts of wealth on your person. Again, this is why food or oil can't be money.

7 **A store of wealth**, the most important point of all. Money *has to be* a store of wealth over *long* periods of time. No exceptions.

This is why currency can never be money. Currency matches only six of the seven points. It can't be a store of wealth over long periods of time because it is often relatively fragile compared to, say, gold and silver and it doesn't last too long. Most paper notes last barely five years in circulation before ending up in tatters. Currency also tends to be in low denominations and notes for efficiency purposes. Gold and silver aren't ideal for everyday use as currency, but civilizations throughout time have had their currency backed by gold or silver.

Put it this way: would you rather find an ancient shipwreck full of gold coins and bars or a shipwreck full of ancient paper currency notes? You'd pick the gold, of course. Gold is universal and has the ultimate fungibility. You would struggle to buy a loaf of bread in other countries with a £5 sterling note but you'd have no problem with gold.

Another reason why currencies can't store wealth over long periods is because currency issued by governments or countries has a short shelf life. Governments can be overthrown; countries can disappear. In those situations, the currency becomes useless. More importantly, governments ruin the purchasing power of their currencies by printing more of it. Zimbabwe is a perfect example of this. Its government tried to inflate the country's national debts away by printing more and more Zimbabwean dollars until it had 89.7 sextillion per cent hyperinflation! This is what it looks like: 89 700 000 000 000 000 000 000 per cent. That's a lot of zeros. Ultimately, the Zimbabwean dollar died and the US dollar took over.

In a nutshell, the key difference between money and currency is that currency is everything money is, except for the fact that it cannot be a store of wealth over long periods of time.

Currencies can't be trusted as they always lose purchasing power the moment the government decides to print more currency to pay debts. That is why gold and silver have a good 5,000-year track record and have kept their value because governments can't just print more gold or silver. Only gold and silver can be money. Nothing else. Not diamonds or oil. Just bullion. It's the only thing that has a track record and is proven, regardless of what happens on the planet.

Are cryptocurrencies money?

No. Hell, the term has 'currencies' in it. Cryptos will be a huge paradigm shift in finance over the next couple of decades, but you can't fool yourself and think that there won't be times of mass horror in the future – whether it's a thermonuclear war, a biological outbreak like the one Bill Gates keeps warning us about, or even the very real threat of AI.

Either way, if disaster strikes, it's unlikely that you will have easy access to a laptop and an Internet connection. You could be a crypto billionaire and it still wouldn't buy you a loaf of bread in a collapsed society without electricity. In times like this, physical gold and silver always become the safest bet again. Bitcoin and cryptocurrencies can never be true money. A crypto may appear that is 'backed by gold' or 'backed by the IMF SDR' (explained later), but it can never be money, only currency.

The point is that even though I'm a massive advocate of cryptos and I'm all in on cryptos in many ways, you should always maintain the big picture. No matter how connected the world becomes, crypto wealth is not real wealth. So when your cryptos finally turn into seven or eight figures, simply convert your newfound riches into real physical assets like land.

The Colonna family perfectly illustrates this point. It's not very well known, but the Colonna family in Italy is one of the oldest (if not the oldest) billionaire families on the planet. They've been relative billionaires for over 930 years and 13 generations. They've survived two world wars, the Black Death, Spanish influenza and many other horrible times. So what is their technique? How on earth have they managed to survive those events and also ensure that their offspring don't squander their wealth away? It's simple. A Colonna family member recently shared their secret: 'A third a third a third'.

They divide their wealth as follows: a third into land (not necessarily property), a third into gold and silver bullion, and a third into fine (museum-quality) art. They have developed this strategy over troubled times throughout history. Whenever they saw the marauders approaching on the horizon, they would quickly roll up their art, get the deeds to their land, load up the horses with bullion and ride off to a safe house. When the threat had finally left, they would simply go back to their villa, pop the art back on the walls, put the bullion back in their safe and reclaim their land with the deeds.

The simple secret is to buy stuff that lasts, and who are we to argue with that? Success leaves clues, so I'm definitely heeding their wisdom!

3
Who created cryptos, and why?

'A cryptocurrency (or crypto currency) is a digital asset designed to work as a medium of exchange using cryptography to secure the transactions. A defining feature of a cryptocurrency, and arguably its most endearing allure, is its organic nature; it is not issued by any central authority, rendering it theoretically immune to government interference or manipulation.'

Wikipedia

In essence, cryptocurrency is just digital currency. It is currency that exists solely on the Internet and completely bypasses any middlemen – in other words, the banks. So I could send money directly to you into your own crypto wallet in a matter of seconds, with negligible, if not zero, transaction fees, and without anyone tracking or watching the transaction.

It's every anarchist's dream, which is why it was no surprise that when Bitcoin, the first mainstream crypto, entered the scene, the black market loved it. Bitcoin's widespread adoption by the more nefarious elements in society in the early days is one of the reasons it grew so much in price to begin with. And we all know what humans are like when they see something zooming up in price. Flushed with FOMO (fear of missing out), we flock to it.

> Economics 101, or basic economics: whenever capital flows into an asset, the price increases.

However, it's important to understand that there's a difference between digital currencies and cryptocurrencies. In the past we have had all sorts of attempts to create a digital currency that uses the Internet to speed up transactions. From eCash and Digi Cash in 1990, to WebMoney in 1998, none of them evidently went mainstream. The only exception is PayPal, with its ability to email transactions over the web.

The real reason why digital currencies never took off is that they were all centralized, in the sense that there was a middleman running the show, and when you have someone else in the picture, there's third-party counter-risk. For example, if you had a lot of money with a certain system like PayPal and it went bust, you'd lose your money. Then you'd have to go through the rigmarole of claiming on insurance. Granted, that's no different from traditional banks, but they've cleverly convinced the public that they are too big to fail.

A cryptocurrency, then, is a form of digital currency, but it often comes with a decentralized system using a blockchain (which we'll cover later). In addition, there is inherent safety built into these currencies as they are encrypted with cryptographic puzzles that computers have to crack. With Bitcoin, for example, the in-built cryptographic security is so good that the National Security Agency spent six months trying to hack it before giving up. And the NSA is the USA's spying organization with near-unlimited resources!

4
How does a crypto have value?

The question of how a crypto has value is a tricky one and there's no single, correct answer, just many converging theories that apply to cryptos. In a nutshell, there are four main reasons:

1 Market perception
2 Scarcity
3 Capital in-/outflows
4 Speculation.

Market perception

What gives anything value? Speak to an economist and they'll bombard you with a number of different variables, but it all comes down to what someone else is prepared to pay for it.

I experience this every day in my private equity company. I like investing in, and buying, other businesses, and so I have a lot of meetings with business owners. I constantly encounter 'entrepreneur delusion', where business owners who have set up, run and grown their business from scratch overvalue the business they've built as a result. Just as every parent believes their baby is the cutest on the planet, the same goes for business owners. I've seen some preposterous valuations, all because the owner can't separate the effort they've put into building it from its actual value.

The main form of value comes from the marketplace or, in other words, what other people deem a fair price. This is one reason why many crypto scams out there fail at the first 'value hurdle'. For example, there is a prominent scam coin called OneCoin. Over 2 million people have been lured into investing in it, but it has no market. The coins' selling price represents nothing more than the price the scheme's owners have set for it. The coin itself is worthless. If it ever did go on to the open market, the price would plummet by 99 per cent on the first day. This is an example of a Ponzi scheme and it will inevitably fail.

Scarcity

Scarcity is another way things derive value. Gold is a classic example of this. Why does gold have any value? There are many reasons, which we will discuss later, but scarcity is a big one; gold is extremely hard to find and mine. Throughout the ages, the amount of gold mined roughly correlates with human population growth at 2 per cent per year. It's because we find it special, and it's so rare, that it has value.

Scarcity is one of the main factors cryptos use to gain value. Most cryptos launch with a limit on the number of coins that will ever exist, so scarcity is built in. For example, in Bitcoin's case, there will only ever be 21 million Bitcoins in existence. And Bitcoin's algorithm is designed to increase its mining difficulty every time a new coin is mined. The very last Bitcoin will be mined in 2140!

Capital in-/outflows

One of the basic rules of the markets is that if capital flows into a specific asset, with all things being equal, the price will soak it up and rise. On the flip side, if capital flees an asset, prices tumble.

We've all seen and felt this first hand since 2008. From 2008 to 2012 the USA more than quadrupled its currency supply, and it didn't stop there. What happened to that extra capital? Despite the objective for that newly created currency being to get it to the general public in order to spark economic growth, it didn't. It never does. What happened was that it was absorbed and funnelled into the equity markets (stocks) and spilled over into the property market. As you can guess, prices for pretty much everything in those two sectors rose dramatically. Of course stocks have gone up. Trillions of dollars are sloshing around, pumping it up.

The main reason cryptos have increased so much in price since 2017 is that a monumental amount of capital has been flowing in, ballooning prices. It's a big wave of capital pushing everything up – even the scammy coins with no real-world utility.

Put it this way. At the beginning of 2017 the total crypto market cap was just $17.7 billion and $15.5 billion of that was in Bitcoin. The price of one Bitcoin was $963. Fast-forward just nine months and the total crypto market cap has ballooned to $190 billion, with $115 billion in Bitcoin. The price of one Bitcoin now stands at $7,000! That's the power of capital inflows.

I'll bet my entire net worth that the price will continue to grow. I'm expecting the crypto market cap to sail far beyond $1 quadrillion within ten years. Just imagine what the prices for all cryptos will be by then.

Speculation

This leads nicely to the topic of speculation. As you can imagine, FOMO (fear of missing out) brings out the worst in amateur investors. They see statements like 'Cryptos are going to grow 10, 100, 1,000 times' and they bet the farm.

Speculation like this fuels volatile price fluctuations, so much so that in many cases the price of a crypto will rally, as 'the market' (that's us) gets so enthusiastic about a particular crypto's potential that the price rises in anticipation of what it's going to do over the next few years. What then happens is nothing, or even a steady and sustained decline, as amateur investors get impatient and lose faith.

Summary

These, then, are the four basic reasons why cryptos have value.

I'm expecting cryptos and blockchain tech to assimilate and infiltrate every aspect of life and the world in the future, but I'm well aware that this is not going to be a smooth ascent. We will see many bubbles, and many bubbles popping. Over time, though, it will increase and become embedded in society. I mean, can you remember what the world was like without the Internet? I can't. I barely remember what I did with all my idle time as a teenager before Facebook popped up!

By the time my son is 16, the term 'cryptocurrency' will no longer be a 'thing'; it'll just be 'money'.

Key advice

Do not risk more than you can afford to lose.
I'm going to say this again because this market will be full of continuous booms and busts:

Do not risk more than you can afford to lose.
If you lose it all, you want to be able to say, 'Oh well, that was fun!' The golden rule is to **use only risk capital**.

5
Risk capital vs moonshot money vs risk cashflow

If you've spent any time in the markets, you'll be aware of the term 'risk capital'. It's a phrase people pay lip service to while completely ignoring it, in the same way that most of us accept T&Cs without actually reading them. I want to shine a spotlight on this term, and its lesser-known sister, risk cash flow, because it's this beauty that has enabled me to load up on high-yielding assets in the past without affecting my total risk too much.

Risk capital

Simply put, risk capital is the portion of your capital that you don't mind losing. It's the amount of your portfolio that, if you did lose it, wouldn't dent your net worth or make you cry in the foetal position, slowly rocking yourself to sleep. You may think I'm joking but I've been close to that and I know a lot of other people who have, too. That is why educating yourself is so important.

Obviously, everyone has a different risk appetite, so you can't cookie-cut a set percentage for risk capital. The super-cautious may say 5 per cent, whereas the more audacious may say 20 per cent. Most would probably gently nod in agreement at 10 per cent.

What that means is that if you had a total of £10,000 to invest, your risk capital would be £1,000. You can do a lot with that, and put it in the unholiest of investments if that's the way you want to play it. After all, this portion of your portfolio is not going to dramatically hurt you financially, or more importantly, emotionally, right?

Moonshot money

Moonshot money isn't an official term but it accurately describes a certain bank account I have and it's a strategy you might find useful, too.

Out of all my bank accounts, my moonshot account is the one that excites me the most. You see, I'm psychologically the *worst* person to be an investor. Investors need to be cold, calm, emotionless and Terminator-like. I have a wild side and a tiny gambling streak that I've spent the last 13 years trying to lasso in. This is one of the coping mechanisms I've come up with to enable me to invest and trade like the Terminator and at the same time keep my portfolio and trading risk-free … from me!

I created moonshot money as a trading safety measure back in 2012 by dividing my trading account in two: my DIY pension super-safe account with no silliness whatsoever; and my moonshot account. Whenever I saw a trade that was a no-brainer, I'd place the normal low-risk trade through my super-safe account, and then go all-in on that trade through my moonshot account.

I only ever put £5,000 in the moonshot account and I end up blowing it up a handful of times every year. Every now and then, though, I run it up to £50 k or more, crystallize a few grand for spending money and then syphon off the rest of the profits into the safe account, leaving the moonshot account at £5,000.

Whether or not you're like me, you might want to use this trick of splitting up your risk capital, too. Using the previous example, where we had £1,000 as risk capital, you could apportion 50 per cent of that (£500) as your moonshot money. The simple objective with this money is to take the big risk and strike a jackpot.

The hit rate from this strategy is low, but you only need to hit it big a handful of times in your life and you're golden. Personally, I'm prepared to accept a 1 per cent hit rate because, with moonshot money, I only swing at crazy investments where the reward more than compensates for the poor hit rate.

Risk cash flow

Risk cash flow is my favourite. It's a term that's widely over-looked and very few people are familiar with it. Risk cash flow is the surplus you're willing to chance on risky invest-ments from your monthly income.

For example, if you take home £2,000 a month and you're left with £500 after all outgoings, that is your monthly sur-plus. It's totally up to you how much of that you are willing to risk. Personally, I take 80 per cent of my surplus and allocate it to investments, siphoning off 20 per cent of it as my risk cash flow. So with a £500 per month surplus, I'll take £400 for general investing with £100 as risk cash flow for the riskier investments.

I apply the same principles to the surplus monthly profits from my businesses, which means that with seven companies I'm able to extract quite a lot of risk cash flow per month for investments like cryptos. An added benefit to risk cash flow is that it will help you pound/dollar cost average your way into a juicy asset or crypto.

Before moving on to the next chapter, grab a piece of paper and work out what risk percentages you are comfortable with and what that means to you in real terms. Once you've done this exercise, you will have far more clarity about how much money you have to invest in cryptos.

6

What on earth is blockchain?

Until the early nineteenth century, a people in Micronesia known as the Yapese had an unusual monetary system, one that can be used to easily explain our modern-day blockchain concept. The island of Yap doesn't have any limestone, and so around 500 CE the Yapese brought limestone to the island from abroad. Due to its rarity, it quickly became a valued commodity and their monetary supply. What they did was drill holes into the centre of flat circular limestone discs and call them *rai* stones.

These stones varied in size: most of them were rather big and weighed as much as a car. They became Yap's main store of value, much like gold. Many smaller transactions still required bartering, but when it came to big purchases like a wedding dowry or paying large debts, the Yapese would trade stones or parts of stones. And this is the fascinating part: whenever a part or a whole *rai* stone was traded, there were no written documents; the acknowledgement of the ownership of the stone was simply relayed to everyone. If person A sold his big *rai* stone to person B, they would both simply tell the whole village and that would be that.

There's even a fabulous story of how a large *rai* stone was lost at sea during a storm. The sailors survived to tell the story and all the Yapese agreed that the stone was still valid and they continued using it as part of their monetary supply, even though it was at the bottom of the ocean. They were still using and swapping ownership of that stone for hundreds of years, despite the fact that no one had seen it.

This is exactly how a blockchain works. You have a network of nodes acting in the same way as members of a Yapese village. Whenever a transaction occurs, every node in the network is informed, a consensus is made and they all agree that the transaction is valid. That transaction is then approved and figuratively carved in stone.

As a result, blockchain forms an almost impenetrable security from bad actors. If someone were to commandeer a node and rewrite the code to send a transaction to a different address, it wouldn't work. A vast number of other nodes would know that it was incorrect and the bad actor would just be ignored.

Obviously, this is blockchain in its simplest form, but you really don't need to understand it in any more detail than that.

Security

This is why Bitcoin is so utterly secure. In order to hack Bitcoin or any other similar blockchain, you would need to hack every single node on the planet at exactly the same time. And there are tens of nodes all over the world, not to mention that Bitcoin uses a military-grade 256-bit secure hash algorithm. In its simplest sense, this means that, in order to hack it, you need to guess a 256-bit sequence of 1s and 0s. Your computer would need to compute around 6.55×10^{76} guesses to crack that 256-bit code. That's 6.5 followed by 76 zeros! Until quantum computing is finally solved, it's totally unfeasible for even our best supercomputers, which is why the National Security Agency (NSA) gave up.

Centralized vs decentralized

There's a bit of confusion about who owns blockchains. As Bitcoin was the first proper crypto out there using a decentralized blockchain, the world quickly, and incorrectly, believed that all blockchains were decentralized. This definitely isn't the case.

To understand what a decentralized blockchain is, we first need to properly understand what a centralized system is. Let's have a look at the US monetary system. It's a centralized system, as is the whole current financial system, because someone, and something, owns and controls it – in this case, the US Central Bank, the Federal Reserve. Whenever the US Government wants more currency (let's say to fund a war), it takes out a loan from the Federal Reserve. The Federal Reserve then types zeros into a computer and invents and creates new currency out of thin air.

Over the years, the Federal Reserve has 'lost' many trillions of dollars, with no explanation of where they went or when. It has never been audited and refuses to open its doors. What's even more shocking is that the Federal Reserve is a private company with private shareholders that earn 8 per cent dividends per year. Spookier still is that its most closely guarded secret is the identity of the shareholders. No one knows but them. Even when roasted by senators in Congress to reveal shareholder identities, representatives of the Federal Reserve wouldn't. You really don't need to believe in the Illuminati because the plain facts about the 'Fed' are just as ridiculous.

The Federal Reserve can create trillions of dollars from nothing and, if the US Government is struggling to repay it, it can lend more money to pay off older debts. The United States is a debt slave to a private organization.

Apologies for the slight tangent; I could have explained this whole section by saying that a centralized system is when someone or something controls it, and that a decentralized system, like the Bitcoin network, has no owners or controllers. It's like an open-source ledger where the community runs and maintains it. The dollar, the pound and any other currency you can think of are all centralized currencies. Bitcoin is not.

Blockchains can be centralized or decentralized. As we'll see in the next chapter, neither one of these is necessarily good or bad.

7
What is Bitcoin mining?

Many aspects of Bitcoin echo the core characteristics of gold. Gold is scarce, hard to mine and a great store of value. Bitcoin emulates these traits as best it can. It's scarce, as only 21 million Bitcoins will ever exist, it's hard to mine, and it has quickly become a great store of digital value in this ever-progressing digital world.

Mining can be a weird concept to get your head around but, before ploughing into it, we're going to go into a bit of background using the Bitcoin network as an example.

Blocks

Every time a transaction is made, the details of that transaction get stored in a block. Every ten minutes we have a new block filled with all the transactions made during that ten-minute period. Imagine holding a bucket under an ice dispenser for ten minutes and every ice cube dispensed being a transaction. At the end of that ten-minute window, the bucket would be sealed and replaced with a new bucket. Each bucket (or block) is then added to the chain of buckets before it, thereby creating a blockchain.

Now imagine that this blockchain is simply a spreadsheet that details a big list of blocks: open source, decentralized, transparent and immutable. That's the basics of blocks and a blockchain. Currently, Bitcoin blocks are 1 megabyte in size and contain an average of 2,000 transactions.

Rewarding the miners

This is where the miners come in. They act as auditors. They go through every single transaction and verify it. But in order to motivate people to verify and keep the blockchain audited and functioning, you have to reward them. The way this works is that every block has a password and whoever comes up with the closest guess within a ten-minute timeframe wins the block and gets rewarded.

The creator(s) of Bitcoin wanted to make it a scarce and a deflationary asset like gold, so they programmed the Bitcoin algorithm to decrease the reward paid out for each mined block over time. At the start, the reward was 50 Bitcoins per block, but it halves every four years. As of November 2017 the reward is 12.5 Bitcoins. The algorithm will get harder and harder, with ever-decreasing rewards until the last Bitcoin is mined in the year 2140.

This is a bit like me writing down a number between 1 and 1,000, putting it in an envelope with 12.5 BTC (Bitcoins), then giving a group of friends ten minutes to guess the number. They can have as many guesses as they like and, at the end of the ten minutes, whoever guesses it first, or gets closest, wins. The guess has to be either equal to or lower than the actual number to count. In the event of a draw, whoever made the most guesses and put the most work in wins the reward. It's called a 'proof of work' system and it's extremely energy-intensive.

Back in the real world, miners have to guess a 64-digit hexadecimal password – in other words, a password that includes numbers and digits and looks something like this: *0000000000000000032frc108cf6130q99i27c5702303e-1w169tt50m7pl3338eb*. As you can imagine, it takes a lot of computing power to guess something like this and, as time goes by, it's becoming increasingly difficult to be a profitable miner unless you have an expensive, fully dedicated mining rig. A mining rig is basically a large number of specially designed single-purpose GPUs that just crunch numbers in order to guess as many combinations as possible. The biggest cost is electricity. It burns through it and the rig produces a lot of heat, so you need to spend more on cooling equipment to prevent it from burning itself out. That's why so many of the world's biggest mining operations are either done in cold countries like Iceland or in areas where electricity is cheap, either through government subsidies or hooked into renewable energy plants like dams and wind turbines. Gone are the days where you could mine a few hundred Bitcoin from your laptop.

8

Bitcoin dominance and the school of 'hard forks'

A centralized crypto isn't necessarily a bad thing and a decentralized crypto isn't necessarily good. Decentralization brings its own problems. Because Bitcoin and other cryptos are decentralized, there is no leader or head honcho calling the shots, which leaves them open to disagreements and attacks. There's a constant Bitcoin civil war going on behind the scenes, which in my opinion will ultimately lead to the death of Bitcoin.

Blockchain is a software-based technology, which means that every now and then it needs upgrading. Some changes are insignificant, like a trivial update that all the miners agree to, referred to as a 'soft fork'. It's a bit like implementing tiny new rules within the existing box of old rules.

FIGURE 8.1 Adding a few new rules to the box of old rules – a 'soft fork'

Occasionally, though, the community gets into a heated debate over the direction of the blockchain. Some may want radical upgrades to ensure that it remains relevant in the world, and some may want to maintain the status quo. This is where a decentralized system falls down, especially in an environment like Bitcoin where so many passionate people are involved.

If 51 per cent of the miners agree to implement a new improvement or adjustment to the blockchain and 49 per cent oppose it, it's called a 'hard fork'. When a 51 per cent attack happens and the community is split on the direction of the blockchain, you get a 'chain split'.

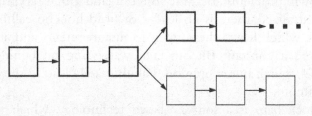

FIGURE 8.2 A chain split

It's akin to having a whole new box of rules that incorporates just some of the old rules.

FIGURE 8.3 New rules incorporating a few of the old rules – a 'hard fork'

The Ethereum 'hard fork'

A classic example of this is the Ethereum and Decentralized Autonomous Organization (DAO) debacle. The DAO was an organization with the objective of providing a decentralized business model for organizing businesses using Smart Contracts. What made it interesting was that it had no management team and was totally open source. The visionaries behind it at the time imagined that it could pave the way to a country with no government, where the people themselves were the government.

The DAO did a successful fund raise and collected just over $150 million from 11,000 investors. All was looking good until a hacker stole $55 million worth of Ether. Despite numerous anti-hacking attempts to retrieve it, no one has been caught. Vitalik Buterin, the founder of Ethereum, and other big movers in that crypto, elected to implement a hard fork in order to patch over any gaps to prevent further hacks. That chain split resulted in two currencies emerging where before there had only been one: Ether Classic (ETC) and the new Ether (ETH).

The Bitcoin cash fork

Although the Ethereum fork was controversial, most people agreed with it. The Bitcoin cash fork, however, is a different story. This hard fork caused physical fights to break out among developers and miners. Essentially, this is a crypto civil war between the West, which favours the original Bitcoin (BTC), and the East (mainly China), which supports Bitcoin Cash (BCH).

The ongoing Bitcoin argument is simple. Bitcoin is great (both parties at least agree on this), but it's woefully inadequate for scaling. Put it this way: Bitcoin can do a maximum of only seven transactions per second. This pales in comparison to VISA, which regularly processes over 24,000 transactions per second. Most people would agree that, for it to properly replace existing financial infrastructure like VISA, a crypto needs to have at least the same capacity.

The bottleneck with this scaling issue is down to block size. Miners mine one block every ten minutes, and there are

1,800–4,200 transactions in each block. BTC has a 1-megabyte block size and a large part of the community wanted to upgrade it to 8 megabytes per block, making it eight times more scalable and giving it a better chance of becoming the crypto of global transactions.

Eventually, Bitcoin Cash supporters won and, on 1 August 2017, Bitcoin experienced its first hard fork. The cool thing for BTC investors was that, if you owned BTC during the fork, you were instantly credited with an identical amount of BCH. This was literally history in the making and no one knew for sure what would happen, so I dramatically reduced my BTC holdings to 1 BTC during the fork. After the fork, I had 1 BCH – which plummeted from its inception price of $550 to $230 within a few days. Nevertheless, this whole drama had set a precedent, and what the general market took away from it was that Bitcoin could be forked and you would be automatically gifted 'free currency'!

Can you guess what then happened? Groups across the world saw this gravy train and attempted to drum up support for more forks under the banner of improvement, when everyone knew they were nothing more than 'pump and dump' schemes.

The first contentious hard fork which many in the community deemed as fishy was Bitcoin Gold. The developers who pushed BTG through knew that they could create this new version of BTG out of thin air and make instant profit. For example, if you held 10 BTC, the moment BTG went live, you would also receive 10 BTG for free. When BTG launched, it was priced at $384, so you would instantly be $3840 in profit. However, because the general crypto community believed it was a 'money-grab', the price of BTG fell continuously. By early 2018 it had fallen to $73 and is likely to continue falling as it has no real-world value or utility. So people will continue to sell it.

There was a failed hard fork called the Segwit2x fork and, right now, I'm hearing plans for Bitcoin Diamond, Bitcoin Silver, Bitcoin Plus and so on. They may as well just be called Bitcoin Printing and Bitcoin Press, because that's all they are. The community have found a legal way to effectively create new currency out of thin air and then sell it straight away for BTC or USD.

Bitcoin may be the very first crypto, the one that carved its way into the history books, but I don't think it's THE ONE. The Bitcoin brand has taken a dent with these forks, and even if they do figure out the scaling difficulty, it has way too many problems.

The big issue for me is that Bitcoin is one of the most wasteful things on the planet. Even though Bitcoin is virtual and is nowhere and everywhere, it has very serious consequences to the planet in the form of energy consumption. Right now, processing every single BTC transaction consumes the same amount of electricity as the average US household uses in a week. It uses more energy per year than the whole of Nigeria! A little piece of my soul dies every time I press send and ping some Bitcoin around the net. Ultimately, this is all unsustainable, unless solar technology rapidly advances or the Bitcoin network changes.

Just as in the tech bubble we had powerhouses like Altavista, Netscape and AOL, which subsequently popped and disappeared after the bubble, Bitcoin may do the same when this bubble eventually implodes. The Facebook, Amazon and Google of the crypto world have not been born yet but it won't be long before they do emerge.

For a true crypto to rule supreme, it needs to be infinitely scalable and Earth-friendly.

Since I've been rather scathing of Bitcoin in this chapter, in the interests of balance I'd like to state that I'm not a hater. As much as I am loath to admit it, I'm a fence-sitter. I personally don't own any Bitcoin now as it's getting to look close to falling (temporarily), and although everyone is raving about how it went up 1,000 per cent in 12 months (November 2016 to November 2017), it's pretty average in terms of performance compared with many other cryptos.

There's also a part of me that thinks that a forked version isn't the answer and that we already have the best version – BTC. I think it's silly to try and scale up this product to compete with the likes of VISA. BTC should be like digital gold. Gold in the real world is finite, clunky, tricky to store and very illiquid. BTC can easily be all of these things. In fact, it already is: it's simply the global reserve crypto currency, just like the US dollar.

Another thing that nearly everyone forgets when touting all these fancy new coins is that no coin or token can become the crypto number one until all the dozens of main exchanges unanimously agree that another coin becomes the 'quote currency'. You see, in currency trading, you can never trade just one currency. You have to trade it against something else. For example, you may want to buy the dollar because you think it's going up, but up against what? It may be going up again the pound but falling against the euro.

It's exactly the same with cryptos, except that, unlike in the foreign exchange markets where you have multiple quote currencies, in cryptos BTC is pretty much the only quote currency. You can buy a few coins with Ether but the selection is limited. To do anything, historically, you needed BTC. If you wanted to buy some altcoins, you couldn't just buy them with pounds Sterling or other fiat currencies (that is, mainstream currencies backed by a government); you had to convert them into BTC, then go shopping with your BTC, and, finally, when you wanted to realize some of your profits from the altcoins, you'd then have to convert them back to BTC, before converting back to fiat. Until all the exchanges agree that a new crypto is the new quote currency, BTC will continue to reign supreme. However, it's highly likely that from 2018 onwards, there will be dozens of exchanges popping up where you can buy pretty much any crypto straight from a fiat currency. In an ideal world it would be handy to see Binance, the world's biggest exchange, allow you to convert fiat currencies into cryptos and back.

To make matters more complicated, for commercial reasons all exchanges would need to agree on a new quote currency at the same time. Crypto exchanges make their money from the small transaction fees they take on every transaction. Volume is everything for them. If one exchange made their main quote currency something other than BTC and the other exchanges didn't follow suit, people would stop using that exchange and kill their cash flow.

At the same time, the exchanges are benefiting from this whole pantomime/war between BTC and BCH as it's causing millions of people to flip-flop between them and generating huge commissions for the exchanges in the process.

9
What's the difference between altcoins and tokens?

If you google 'cryptos', you'll see the terms alt(ernative) coins and tokens a lot. Most of the time they are incorrectly blurred into the same thing. As we've established, cryptos are simply digital currencies that are governed and secured by cryptography. Bitcoin was the first horse out of the gates with this new asset class, and, as it was a digital currency that incorporated cryptography, the term 'cryptocurrency' was born.

Bitcoin's wild success set off a chain of events that sparked an explosion of development in this industry. As such, it wasn't long before other cryptos appeared, and there's now a vast array of different types of crypto, each with its associated ecosystem. Unfortunately, because nearly every new crypto that emerged for the first few years was a copycat cryptocurrency, the term has stuck and now people obliviously use it when referring to all sorts of crypto. It's a bit like calling all vehicles a 'car', which is incorrect. The first internal combustion engine vehicle was a car, and after the car industry took off there were all sorts of variants being created – vans, lorries, trucks and motorbikes, among them. So, using the term 'cryptocurrency' when referring to the general crypto market is an incorrect blanket term. This is why I use the term 'cryptos', as it covers all crypto-based assets whether it's a currency or not.

But getting back to the topic of the difference between 'altcoins' and 'tokens', we should first look at the word 'coin'. In simple terms, a coin is historically a metal circular disc that has been used to transfer value from one party to another. But a coin hasn't always been a metal disc as there have been civilizations that have used stones, wood, gems, emeralds and diamonds for the material and squares, triangles and rectangles for the shape. The key defining trait of a 'coin' is the fact that it transfers value from one to another. So, the basic definition of an altcoin is any cryptocurrency (other than Bitcoin) that transfers value. But there's slightly more to it than that because we also have to see whether it's a free-standing crypto or a crypto based on another platform.

Since 2017 there has been an explosion of crypto platforms that help people build their own cryptos (just like WordPress is a website-building platform). These are referred to as DApp platforms – decentralized app platforms, and prominent examples are Cardano, NEO and Ethereum. So when someone creates a crypto based on one of these DApp platforms, these are referred to as tokens. These tokens are used to transfer information and/or value. So one could argue that there are cryptos out there based on a DApp platform which are also transfers of value, but the easy way to look at them is like air miles. If a new airline wanted to have an air miles system, they could simply sign up to an air miles system like Avios and then their customers could accrue Avios air miles points.

Perhaps an easier way to get your head around it is by looking at web page builders like wix.com. Wix is a simple platform where you can use their templates to very quickly create a simple, nice-looking website or landing page. But we all know that you don't really have a proper website if it's created by Wix because your site is not a free-standing website as it relies on Wix. What would happen if Wix went bankrupt, or its servers got broken or hacked? Your Wix website wouldn't load. So, continuing with this analogy, an altcoin is like a proper free-standing website not based on a third-party platform, and a token is like a website that is based upon a third-party platform like Wix.

> Typically, a token is a crypto that is built upon another platform and an altcoin is historically a crypto that transfers value.

There are also companies now trying to 'tokenize' their business in order to raise capital – in other words, do a crypto cash-grab. So people then 'invest' into these projects and are issued tokens which represent a share or stake in that company or project. Even though you can sell those tokens later, as you could with any normal share, it's not a currency. The token in this instance is a digital representation of the underlying asset. So, in this case, projects/cryptos like this would be classed as a token, not an altcoin.

You now know the two main points that determine the difference between tokens and altcoins. Let's add something else into the mix. There are also many cryptos out there which are free-standing cryptos but are not designed to be cryptocurrencies. So what would you call these? An altcoin or token? Which determining factor takes priority, the transfer of value or whether it's free-standing or not? Personally, I feel that the industry has progressed to the point that we just can't have two pigeonholes for cryptos anymore. In this example, I would call a free-standing crypto which isn't a transfer of value a tokenized asset/security.

> As time progresses, we need to move away from having just two types of classification. And if you come across a crypto that is more like a stock, then it's most likely a tokenized asset/security.

10
Getting to grips with the different crypto sectors

Many people still think that Bitcoin is the only cryptocurrency out there. It would be nice and simple if that were the case, but it's not. Pretty much everything about cryptos is fiddly, and there hundreds of new cryptos popping up every year. Just as stocks have different sectors (tech and pharmaceutical, for example), there is now a plethora of different crypto sectors, too, and this is just the start.

Currently, these are the main crypto sectors:

- Currency
- General-purpose platform
- Distributed storage
- Distributed computation
- Shitcoins
- Privacy
- Prediction markets
- Identity
- Advertising
- Time-stamping
- Payment platform
- Exchanges.

It's a bit of a funfair, isn't it? Let's briefly have a look at each one so you're able to pigeonhole a token when you see one.

Currency

This is an easy one. Currency is the original crypto genre and digital cash has for a long time been the goal of many developers. Bitcoin was the first and many have since followed, like Litecoin, Monero and Dash.

General-purpose platform

This was the next natural development in the crypto world. In the early days of cryptos, the barrier to entry was quite high, so it wasn't long before platforms emerged that helped developers launch their own tokens. Ethereum was the first to gain traction in this sector. Think of these as being like WordPress. Just as WordPress is an engine that enables people to create websites, Ethereum, NEO, Waves, Cardano and so on enable people to launch their own tokens.

Distributed storage

Distributed storage is a Cloud storage killer. Dropbox and Google Drive had better pivot before they lose their market share. The term 'Cloud storage' is a bit misleading, because your data isn't stored online but in a few data centres across a particular country or two. That's fine as long as the data centres are secure, but let's say a war breaks out and they're destroyed. You can say goodbye to your cherished photographs and data.

This is where cryptos like Siacoin, Maidsafe and Storj come in. They are disrupting this industry by enabling users to upload their data to a blockchain, where it's shredded into millions of tiny fragments and stored on computer hard drives all over the world. So your data is everywhere but nowhere, and no individual or group can piece it together. What's even better is that it rewards those who contribute to the network, so you could leave your computer on overnight, for example, and the network will use up a tiny portion of your hard drive and you'll earn tokens as a result.

Distributed computation

This is similar to distributed storage except for computation power. Imagine a doctor or a researcher trying to solve a complex calculation. Until now, if they needed to number-crunch things, they had to go to a specialist university with a supercomputer, which is rather costly. Not any more: cryptos like Golem disrupt this by harnessing the unused power of the public's spare RAM (random access memory). So when you're not using your computer you can hook it up to the network and the network will use a small portion of your computer's RAM, again earning you tokens in the process. It's a brilliant idea because now the public has access to power of a supercomputer for a fraction of the cost.

Shitcoins

There's not much to say here other than that at least 90 per cent of the cryptos out there are just plain stupid. They're either copycats of successful cryptos, promoting a stupid cause or created by people in their bedroom for fun, like Titcoin and Wankcoin. Yes … Earth has reached a new low. The most prolific example of a stupid coin with ZERO real-world utility is Dogecoin. It's a coin with a Shiba Uno dog as its logo, and its community post poor English phrases like 'Much wow' and 'When Moon?' What's staggering is that Dogecoin has a market cap of over $130 million! Long story short, don't waste your time with these shitcoins.

Privacy

These cryptos were created with anonymity and privacy as their main feature and are coins like Monero and Zcash. With Monero, you can transact with complete privacy, with no traceability or linkability. It's no surprise that the black market loves Monero.

There are also non-currency privacy cryptos, like Digital Note. This privacy-protected blockchain offers instant untraceable encrypted messaging. It's a remarkable system and it's surprising how low their market cap is right now. It's definitely one to watch when the black market finds out about this crypto.

Prediction markets

This is a fascinating new industry. There are a few companies out there that make a living by crunching data mined from Twitter, Facebook and other social media networks. By analysing patterns and linguistic trends about a particular topic/matter/event, they can accurately predict the outcome. For example, there's a company in South Africa that accurately predicted Brexit, Trump and a few other outcomes. As a result, they have governments knocking on their doors all the time. Gnosis and Augur are the main prediction cryptos, although they are not like the company I just mentioned. At the moment, they are playing more of a 'market maker' role, so if you think a team will win a football game, you can buy 'shares' in that outcome and be rewarded in tokens if you win.

Identity

Getting verified for things can be a bit of a chore, which is why this small sector is starting to emerge. Identity verification cryptos such as Civic aim to allow you to upload all your relevant information to the blockchain, so that whenever your identity needs verifying you can simply issue a code for any third party to access the information they need. This would speed up the whole verification process greatly as background checks wouldn't then need to start from the ground up every time.

Advertising

Advertising is a new sector that will grow rather fast when cryptos go mainstream, because attention is everything these days. Advertisers pay a lot of money for attention. BAT is a crypto aiming to capitalize on this by creating a token that can be exchanged between publishers, advertisers and users within their network. It's not really an original concept, but watch this space …

Time-stamping

This is a crucial aspect of business and accounting. I'll say this throughout the book: blockchain represents a revolution of trust. What this means is that we no longer need to trust third parties, as everything and anything can be immutably recorded on a blockchain. Factom aims to do just this by providing the world's first verifiable and immutable audit trail. It's perfect for accounting, auditing, system processes, workforce attendance, financial markets, paying transactions and legal documents. Whoever hoovers up the market share in this sector will become a huge business.

Payment platforms

These are exactly what it says: payment platforms for cryptos, the crypto equivalents of PayPal, Worldpay, Stripe and so on.

Players in this space at the moment are Metal, Tenx and Omisego. Metal already has a debit card, which you can load up with cryptos and use for daily transactions. Once cryptos go mainstream this sector will explode, as people will need to be able to pay with and accept cryptos.

Exchanges

Currently there are two types of crypto exchange, those that don't accept Fiat currencies and those that do. The main players that accept Fiat are Coinbase, Kraken and Lykke and there are dozens of non-Fiat-accepting exchanges like Bittrex, Poloniex and Shapeshifter. The basic model for how a crypto exchange token grows in value is due to commissions. An exchange like Binance has a token called Binance Coin (BNB). When users use the exchange and Binance makes their tiny commission per transaction, it increases the tradable value of BNB.

> This is a simple but by no means exhaustive list of the different sectors in this market. As tech and innovation grows, there will be more sectors sliding on to the dance floor but, for now, you're fully briefed on the main ones.

11
The reasons why I originally
disliked cryptos

I'm an entrepreneur and an investor, but my core skill is trading, which I've been doing since 2004. When you become a competent trader, the skills you develop truly change your life. One of the most important is your 'risk radar'.

Proper traders are not spontaneous wild cards who shoot from the hip, but the most calculated and cautious group of people you will find. I like a gamble but, when it comes to my main pot, I'm super-cautious. And having been comprehensively cheated in the markets and in business, I guess I'm more sceptical and cautious than most. Every time I looked at the crypto opportunity between 2009 and 2016, even with solid research, I couldn't justify exposing my hard-earned money to an industry I didn't understand or believe would last. With hindsight, I was sorely mistaken.

I routinely hear a lot of the same concerns I used to have, so here are the seven main reasons that prevented me from pulling that trigger.

1 **It's not a real thing. It doesn't exist anywhere other than the Internet!**
   I'm a big fan of things that last and store value. I'm a bit of a gold and silver geek. Everything about these metals fascinates me – how they are formed, the economics and politics behind them and the fact that they are real. You can see, feel and lick them.

   There's huge commercial and utility use for silver as it's the second most consumed commodity on the planet (oil being the first), and every single electronic device needs silver to function. I accidentally became one of the UK's fastest-growing bullion dealers, all because I just wanted to buy bullion for myself at wholesale prices.

   This was why, when crypto started cropping up, I dismissed it as just an Internet thing. It's everywhere but nowhere, you can't touch it, and the question I kept asking myself was 'What on earth do you do if you lose electricity or access to the Internet?' What would happen if you held a lot of wealth in cryptos and the government decided to crack down on it all and 'do a China'? You'd lose everything, I thought.

It's also definitely not a store of value as it's only really been around since 2009, when Bitcoin launched. At best, I thought it was just another fad Internet currency that would fail because PayPal was already partly fulfilling that role.

2 **It was and still is the biggest bubble in human history.** In 1636 Western Europe experienced 'tulipmania' when, in a very short time, it became very fashionable to own certain tulips, which pushed their price up to extremely high levels. At the peak of this mania, one tulip bulb of the Viceroy variety sold for the following:

- 3.6 tonnes of wheat
- 4 tonnes of rye
- 4 fat oxen
- 8 fat swine
- 12 fat sheep
- 600 litres of wine
- 4,582 litres of beer
- 2 tonnes of butter
- 453 kg of cheese
- A complete bed
- A suit of clothes
- A silver drinking cup.

In today's money, that's worth about $2 million, an absurd price to pay for a simple tulip bulb with no real-world utility. I steered clear because I thought cryptos would be a bigger bubble than tulipmania.

By this time I had done a fair amount of research into cryptos and I felt somewhat vindicated whenever I looked at the statistics for Bitcoin from mid-2013 to mid-2015. It's a perfect example of a bubble. Bitcoin exploded from $80 to $1,160 and then went straight back down to $235. What the 'confirmation bias' part of me failed to compute was that, despite this crazy 'pump and dump', it still bottomed out at around the $250 level – a good 200 per cent increase on where it had been just two years earlier.

3 **Counterparty risk is astronomical.**
Counterparty risk is basically the risk you take, when engaging in business with someone or something else, that the other party won't stick to their obligations. For example, if you keep your money in a bank, there's counterparty risk because the bank could go bust and you could lose your money. If you loan some money to a friend, the counterparty risk is that they may not pay you back.

Pretty much every aspect of investing in cryptos carries some form of risk. When you buy your cryptos you have to send your Fiat currencies to an exchange. There's a real risk that the exchange could go bust or be hacked. Almost every major exchange has already been hacked, as you can see from the list of exchange hacks between October 2011 and April 2017 (Table 11.1). I've been precise with the dates here because it's almost a quarterly occurrence and will no doubt be a lot higher by the time you are reading this.

Date	Exchange	Bitcoins missing
Apr 2017	Yapizon	3,816
Oct 2016	Bitcurex	2,300
Aug 2016	Bitfinex	119,756
May 2016	Gatecoin	250
Mar 2016	CoinTrader	81
Mar–Apr 2016	ShapeShift	469
Mar 2015	Allcrypt	42
Feb 2015	KipCoin	>3,000
Feb 2015	Bter	7,170
Jan 2015	796 Exchange	1,000
Jan 2015	Bitstamp	<19,000
Aug 2014	BitNZ	39
July 2014	Cryptsy	11,325
July 2014	Moolah/Mintpal	>3,700
Mar 2014	Poloniex	97
Feb 2014	Mt. Gox	650,000
Nov 2013	BIPS	1,295
May 2013	Vircurex	1,454
Dec 2012	BitMarket.eu	18,788
Sept 2012	Bitfloor	24,000
July 2012	BTC-e	4,500
July 2012	Bitcoinica	40,000
July 2012	Mt. Gox	1,852
May 2012	Bitcoinica	18,547
Mar 2012	Bitcoinica	43,554
Oct 2011	Bitcoin7	5,000

TABLE 11.1 Thefts from bitcoin exchanges, October 2011 – April 2017. *Sources*: Reuters, Professor Tyler Moore at the University of Tulsa, Crypto Compare and various websites.

The table shows a total of 981,035 Bitcoin stolen. As I write this, BTC is valued at $8,200, which values the stolen Bitcoin at just over $8 billion. There's also the risk of your own crypto wallets or computer being hacked, or of a particular crypto being delisted from an exchange or just dropping to $0. It's a really risky space to be in if you don't know what you're doing and you're not diligent with your personal online security.

Every time I heard of another hacking, my confirmation bias would kick in. As with any 'gold rush', there's mass hysteria and FOMO (fear of missing out) and it doesn't take long for the snakes, charlatans and con artists to set up scams and dodgy MLMs (multi-level marketing) to lure gullible or uninformed victims.

4 The Establishment does not like cryptos.

I believed that the Establishment would find a way to ban cryptos. There's a reason for the saying 'Don't fight the Fed'. I'm using 'Establishment' to cover all the 'elites' out there, such as the banks, central banks, governments and secretive influential families like the Rothschilds, the Rockefellers and the Warburgs.

Simply put, they do not like Bitcoin or what cryptos represent. Most are scared of it, especially the banks. In the grand scale of things, cryptos are a tiny new industry – but one that is seriously prodding an established $100-trillion industry. Everything about the Establishment is being threatened. They aren't just going to roll over and say 'Oh, well. Time to retire ...' They will aim to pivot, hijack, tarnish, own or destroy cryptos with the almost unlimited resources at their disposal.

If the future potential of Bitcoin comes true, it means the death of *all* banks, which is why they are now ploughing billions into blockchain/crypto tech. Nearly every major bank now has a 'blockchain innovation' department, which is simply code for 'We're furiously trying to build our own cryptocurrency to force on to everyone, so we can remain relevant somehow!'

The fear is that the whole reason for the existence of cryptos will be completely lost with these bank attempts. Cryptos were meant to be open, transparent, immutable, decentralized and trustworthy. The moment you create a private crypto/blockchain, it becomes the opposite. Long story short, this crypto vs Establishment war is going to be absolutely fascinating and we all have front-row seats with popcorn.

5 **Top investing rule: don't invest in things you don't understand.**

The rule of investing only in things you understand applies to *all* asset classes, but especially with this Wild Wild West of a market. Far too often, I see on social media people posting things like 'Can someone buy some Bitcoin for me, please?' These people will get bitten eventually. There are literally dozens of things that can go wrong and often do, if you don't know what you're doing. For example, when sending cryptos from one place to another, one small typo and you've lost those coins for ever – there are no rewinds. A good habit to develop when moving things around is just to copy and paste the addresses (Control + C followed by Control + V) to avoid errors.

But the main reason you need to understand this market and the mechanics behind it all is to do with data and wealth security. Nothing teaches you more about data security than being hacked! Suddenly, you become a mini-expert on it out of pure necessity. We spend our lives browsing the web, willingly storing and publishing personal data everywhere, whether it's using the same password for everything, posting on Facebook or not saving back-ups. When you're trying to protect dozens of Bitcoin, you quickly learn!

The last point I'd like to make about this is trust. If you don't know the game you're playing or the rules you're playing by, you're going to be abused. Because if you don't know how to safely buy, store and sell cryptos yourself, you will be forced to trust someone else to do it for you or, even worse, get someone else to buy and store your cryptos on your behalf. If you have the delightful experience of watching your cryptos soar and your investment growing by 10,000 per cent or more (which is quite common now), you'd better hope you trusted the right person.

Also, echoing the previous counterparty risk point, don't be lulled into trusting an exchange that has special 'storage facilities' or, even worse, a bank that offers to store your cryptos. If the UK Government does some day decide to go 'full China' and ban everything, the first place they will look are the exchanges and banks.

Also, don't be lulled into believing 'storage companies' that claim to be insured. They will be insured only up to a small amount and, even if you are fully insured, it will be only for your original investment. A great but shocking example is Mt. Gox. This was the biggest exchange on the planet. It held hundreds of millions of dollars' worth of people's cryptos. Then one day it was hacked. Over 750,000 of their customers' Bitcoins were lost and the exchange subsequently shut down. Bitcoin was trading at around $600 at the time. By November 2017 the investigation and court case was complete and there are two bitter twists to all this. The clients who lost out have been reimbursed only to the amount of their original investment, despite the soaring prices. One victim lost 35 Bitcoin as a result of this debacle but was reimbursed only about $21,000, when his Bitcoin would now be worth well over $280 k!

To rub salt in the wounds, in Japanese law (where this all happened), once all creditors have been paid off in a liquidation, anything remaining goes to the shareholders. And during the investigation they 'found' 200,000 Bitcoin in an old wallet that is now being given back to the founder of Mt. Gox, Mark Karpeles. So if the alleged victims are remunerated with the amount they originally invested, Mr Karpeles could walk away with over $1.6 billion. It should be stressed, however, that, at the time of writing, proceedings against Mr Karpeles are still pending and he has not pleaded guilty, so he could still be exonerated.

Returning to the original point of this section, if you ever find yourself asking 'What should I do with my money?' or 'How do I buy cryptos?', then you're a target for scams.

6 **Bitcoin wasn't and isn't scalable.**
A dilemma I couldn't get my head around in the past was that Bitcoin isn't that scalable. We've already gone over the fact that it can do a maximum of only seven transactions per second, which is woefully inadequate compared to the 24,000 per second that VISA does. And, surely, in order for something to be the new global digital currency, it should at least match VISA, or even the 328 transactions per second that SWIFT (Society for Worldwide Interbank Financial Telecommunication) does?

On average, it takes about 30 minutes to complete a Bitcoin transaction, so I thought there was absolutely no way this crypto could be a daily-use currency. You wouldn't be able to buy a coffee with it if you had to stand and wait half an hour for your money to clear. What I didn't understand at the time is that Bitcoin is not a currency of daily use for the world. It's digital gold and, like gold, it's going to end up being the unofficial global world reserve currency. It will be a foreign currency for everyone and probably the best store of wealth for intermediate periods of time.

7 There is a Bitcoin bottleneck in China.

I'm not a fan of counterparty risk. When I allocate my money to any investment, I need as much control over the outcome and the investment as possible. When looking at who can influence Bitcoin, it turns out that there is a concentration of Bitcoin mining power in China. It's hard to say how much exactly. Reports suggest anything from 50 to 60 per cent of the total network.

The data is slightly old now, but as of 2015 three Chinese miners equated to almost half the world's mining power: Bitmain (the world's largest mining company, which also runs Antpool) accounted for 17.82 per cent of the Bitcoin mining network; DiscusFish had 16.49 per cent; and BTC China Pool had another 13.74 per cent.

My fear was that, if China really, *really* wanted to kill Bitcoin, it could just commandeer or shut down the warehouses of these huge mining companies. If this were to happen, the whole Bitcoin blockchain would be frozen for months while the rest of the world tried to catch up with the backlog of transactions to process. The price of Bitcoin would freeze until the rest of the world could take up the slack and it doesn't take a genius to imagine what would happen to the price of Bitcoin when it went online again.

This held me back from the Bitcoin market for years. It is rather comforting to see that China hasn't done anything of the sort, even when it effectively banned crypto trading against the yuan in October 2017.

12
Understanding the technology adoption curve

For a new emerging technology to gain traction, infiltrate the global markets and do well, it has to attract five key demographics:

- The innovators
- The early adopters
- The early majority
- The late majority
- The laggards.

The demographics looks like this:

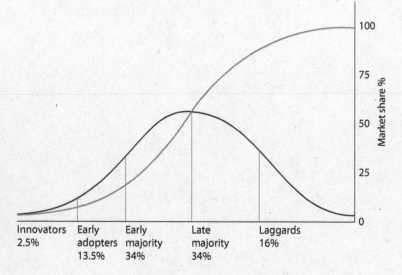

FIGURE 12.1 The new technology adoption curve

This theory originated from a smart chap called Everett Rogers in his 1962 book *Diffusion of Innovations*. At the time it was just a theory, but over the last five decades we have gained empirical data to prove that Rogers was spot on.

In this graph the black curve depicts the market adoption by each sector of people and the paler curve shows us the accumulative market share.

Let's have a look at this curve with Bitcoin in mind, so that you can see how and who will jump on to this train, and when.

The innovators

These are the technology enthusiasts – the geeks and the nerds. After the 2009 Bitcoin White Paper, cryptographers, computer scientists, data security experts, whizz kids and bedroom nerds discovered Bitcoin and began playing with it.

Bitcoin also came around at the end of the 2008 sub-prime mortgage collapse and intense 'currency printing', mainly in the form of quantitative easing (QE). Because of this, it appealed to the anarchists, the anti-establishmentarians, the libertarians and the 'sound money' fans. It was this mixture of people that seeded Bitcoin's early-stage growth by creating the community around it.

Good examples of innovators in other industries would be those Apple fans that queue for days outside stores for a new product, or anyone buying up virtual-reality headsets right now, when the tech still has a long way to go (and, yes, I am one of them).

The early adopters

These are also forward-looking individuals and companies who just 'get it'. They are visionaries, who may be slightly later to the party than the innovators but they understand it straight away and don't need much convincing. A good example of this in the Bitcoin space is the black market; this underground economy quickly identified that it was the perfect currency for their illegal activities and so they helped propel the development of the tech.

The myriad crypto exchanges that have been popping up since 2010 were also early adopters. They saw that this would be a modern-day 'gold rush' and that the easiest way to win in a gold rush would be to sell the spades and buckets instead of doing the digging. They became facilitators for Bitcoin's growth and adoption.

In terms of users, if you start investing in cryptos any time from now till the end of 2018, you can call yourself an early adopter. Even though Bitcoin is currently flirting with the $12,000 level, there's still a lot more potential for growth, as Big Money – banks, institutions, 'Wall Street' – starts to wade in and the public at large remains oblivious.

Other examples of early adopters would be electric car drivers. The electric car infrastructure isn't there yet, but give it five years and we'll have cars that do over 1,000 miles per charge, take under five minutes to fully charge, high performance will be standard, and charge points will be everywhere. Only then will the early and late majority come piling into this market.

The early majority

It's when the early majority jump into a market or tech that the price shoots up. These people are called pragmatists with good reason. They tend to be open-minded, but they'll happily sit on the fence observing a market if they identify inherent drawbacks.

In Bitcoin's case, the early majority are unsure what governments will do about it, and they don't like that it isn't in everyday use for buying their daily coffee or paying taxes or their rent/mortgages with it. This indecision is preventing them from making good profits. When you know a tech is here to stay, capital will continue to flood in. It's as simple as getting your boat into the water and letting the rising tide carry you into easy profits.

The late majority

As you can see from the graph, the majority of people are concentrated in the early and late majority. The late majority absolutely won't get into anything until the early majority have gone in. This group tends to be older and they have all of the same objections as the early majority, except that they are slightly more stubborn and less open-minded. These conservatives won't be jumping into anything until there is absolutely zero risk. In the crypto space, this group will no doubt adopt cryptos once governments have forced their own national crypto on to us.

The laggards

It's fair to say that the laggards are sceptics and will never adopt, or they will only reluctantly come on board. This group is still coming to terms with mobile phones and probably even the Internet.

Converting the early majority

These are the five groups any new tech has to overcome. We are all in one of these groups. From a business perspective, the important thing to learn is that for mass-market adoption, you *have* to convert the early majority. This is the linchpin. There will always be pioneers and visionaries who will find you, but there is a chasm between the early adopters and the early majority that needs to be bridged.

In the crypto space, many hurdles must be overcome before the early majority come on board, but it's already starting to happen and will certainly continue to happen. We are currently seeing hordes of developers and engineers fleeing the banking sector for the crypto space. In addition to that, talent from across different industries is being pulled in, which can only be a good thing. Scientists, cryptographers and IT geniuses created this industry, and it's far too complex for the public as a whole yet. Give it time, though, and businesses will start to drive in the user experience side to make things easier.

13
Understanding the three phases of emerging technologies

It's important to note that although you'll hear many people saying things like 'Blockchain is the new technology behind Bitcoin', this is not exactly the case. Blockchain tech, or distributed ledger tech (DLT), has been around for decades now. So really, Bitcoin *is* the new technology that happens to use a blockchain. In any case, when you have a new disruptive technology out there such as cryptos, they tend to flow through three main stages: punt, speculation and established.

The punt phase

The punt phase is when something bursts on to the scene with visionary potential, just as when Bitcoin and its White Paper were released in 2009. In the punt phase no one has any idea whether a new tech will last two minutes or two years. At this point, only the pioneers and the super early adopters will go near it. Good examples of tech that never moved beyond the punt phase are Betamax, HD-DVD and virtual reality, although, interestingly, VR is making a rapid comeback 20 years later.

In this phase the prices are volatile and it's a high investment risk. Institutions and Big Money won't give it the time of day and people generally dismiss it as a fad. It was like this with the Internet and the internal combustion engine. Bitcoin was in this phase from 2009 until 2016.

The speculation phase

It's a defining moment when a technology enters the speculation phase, as this is when there's a tidal mindset shift towards it as people realize that it isn't a fad and that it's here to stay. At this point, the early adopters pile in trying to accumulate early market share, capital pours in and innovation takes off. Bitcoin, and cryptos as a whole, entered this phase in around mid-2016.

This is the moment when you get the most explosive price action and media air time. There was a prime example of this around 1996 when the Internet was suddenly off to the races, with tech start-ups raising ridiculous amounts of money with no real plan or team. Ultimately, mad rushes like this end with a big popping of the bubble (as with the tech bubble crash of 2000/01), but, believe it or not, it's actually a healthy process for the technology.

Because of the massive amount of capital and talent that is attracted to it, you begin to see fast improvements and, when the tree shakes, only the proper companies are left. The tech is then ready to move into the established phase.

The established phase

The bubble has popped. Everyone is now aware of it. Some people have no doubt been burned but at this stage it's now an established asset class or mainstream tech. When the tech bubble burst it decimated the Internet industry but what was left was an open sky for the technology and a bit more regulation from the authorities. Cryptos aren't there yet, so the bubble still needs to burst.

When cryptos enter the established phase, it will be a mainstream investment asset class in which institutions will have a portion of their capital invested. Speak to most fund or pension managers today about investing in Bitcoin and they'll laugh at you, but give it time and eventually all funds will have an allocation and the whole of Wall Street will have spun their spider web of financial instruments in order to skim off their commissions through things like futures, options, ETFs and other derivatives.

Where are we now?

Right now, we are in the speculation phase and seeing the craziest action and hype. It's the phase I like to enter into an asset because I know it will survive; it's more VHS than Betamax. The greatest possible gains in the shortest possible time come within this phase. Don't be fooled, though: it's *always* going to be a roller coaster of a ride, but don't let this volatility deter you.

This is why you should apply some of your risk capital — and then just sit on it.

14
Understanding bubbles and the standard bubble wave

How would you like to go back in time to 2002 and buy Apple and Amazon stock during the aftermath of the original tech bubble crash? I know I would.

Bubbles fascinate me to the point where I've become a bit of an historian of them. They've happened in every market for as long as markets have existed. The key thing to remember is that, despite the nature of a bubble and the fact that people get burned, they present three of the greatest personal wealth building opportunities out there. These are:

- profiting as it enters exponential growth
- shorting it (profiting as it falls)
- profiting from the slow but beastly rally once the devastation has settled.

There are four distinct phases of the standard bubble wave, as shown in this graph:

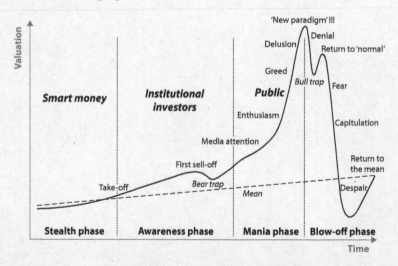

FIGURE 14.1 The four phases of the standard bubble wave. *Source*: Dr Jean-Paul Rodrigue, Dept. of Global Studies and Geography, Hofstra University, Long Island, New York.

1 **The stealth phase**
In this phase, smart and Big Money, billionaires and vision-aries identify an undervalued asset and start to build up a position. For example, in the 1970s the billionaire Bunker Hunt feared the decline of the dollar and started buying up silver at around $6 per ounce. He bought so much that he effectively cornered the market, and by 1980 the price per ounce had spiked to $49.45.

2 **The awareness phase**
Here, other sophisticated investors pick up the crumbs left behind by the big boys and also identify the undervalued asset, and they start to pile in. You'll see a nice increase in prices towards the end of this phase, and it's this increase that acts as a beacon in the sky for the general public.

Cryptos are now reaching the end of this phase. The supermaterial graphene is early on in this phase. Graphene is just one atom thick, tougher than any metal and more flexible than anything. It's so strong that it would take the weight of an elephant on top of a drawing pin to pierce a sheet of graphene the thickness of cling film. Before you get any ideas, it's way too early to invest in. There's no proper commercial application for graphene yet, and they're still figuring out how to make it at scale.

3 **The mania phase**
In this phase the public are like a moth to a flame. As soon as they see news articles about great returns and hear about friends getting rich, a massive pang of FOMO kicks in. Wel-come to the mania phase (which I prefer to call the media phase because a large reason why the public are ploughing in is the noise made in the press and social media). Cryptos are tiptoeing into the mania phase now but it's being held back by an abundance of scams, exchanges crashing and fake news.

Once the exchanges get organized and the whole user experience becomes simpler, that's when it will take off.

4 **The blow-off phase**

It's evident what happens in the blow-off, or dissipation, phase: a lot of people get financially and emotionally wrecked. Right now, cryptos are making the early adopters plenty of money, but I believe this bubble will pop around mid-2019. That's my best guess but a better gauge would be market cap. As it stands, the crypto market capitalization (all the money that is flowing around this open market) is $650 billion. When you compare this against the rest of the world's main markets, it's tiny. Cryptos are $0.65 trillion, gold is $7 trillion, global stocks are $70 trillion, global bonds are $100 trillion and the currency market is the big dog at $1.4 quadrillion. That's $5 trillion per day!

FIGURE 14.2 Global asset market caps: cryptos compared with the rest of the world's main markets (T = trillion; Q = quadrillion)

Cryptos are really insignificant now. My personal crypto portfolio grew from $25 k to $1.1 million in the space of four months, when the market cap shot up from $130 billion to $650 billion. This is happening to people across the globe. Imagine what will happen when some crumbs fall down from the stock and bond markets; a few trillion would barely make a dent in them.

The thing about the standard bubble wave is that it applies to all bubbles. Whether it's cryptos or wheat futures, bubbles can happen anywhere and everywhere. The crypto bubble isn't the only one around at the moment. We have a motor-loan bubble, a student debt bubble, a sovereign debt bubble, a pension bubble, a currency bubble, a bond bubble, a stock bubble and a personal debt bubble. There hasn't been a time in human history with so many concurrent bubbles. The exciting prospect is that all it takes is just one bubble to pop and initiate a chain of events that could pop every other bubble.

15

The lessons and comparisons of the dotcom bubble

I think that cryptos will get to at least $10 trillion before the bubble pops or deflates, and here are a few reasons why:

- All middlemen businesses will eventually be made redundant. We are seeing this wave of decentralization already. Airbnb is the world's biggest hotel company but it doesn't own any hotels; Uber is the world's biggest taxi company but it doesn't own any taxis. Blockchain will eliminate all middlemen, which means that, one day, cryptos will encompass the whole foreign exchange (FX) market because it's a middleman market.

- During times of economic uncertainty, people flee to perceived safe havens such as the dollar, gold and land. During the next banking crisis, cryptos will be added to that list as people stampede away from onerous sovereign regulation or if a country's currency supply fails. Look at what's happening in Venezuela, which is about to hit hyperinflation. It's got to the point where the government is struggling to afford to pay for all the extra notes it's printing and instead is introducing its own crypto, as it's effectively free.

- Most big developed nations have increased their currency supply by an average of 1,228 per cent between 1999 and 2017.

Table 15.1 shows the official statistics:

Country	Percentage increase, 1999–2017
Japan	73%
EU	197%
USA	263%

Country	Percentage increase, 1999–2017
Canada	322%
South Korea	485%
India	1,560%
Brazil	1,814%
China	2,760%
Russia	3,580%

TABLE 15.1 Increase in currency supply in key countries or trading blocs

There's now at least 12 times more currency in the system than there was during the original tech bubble of 1997–2000/2001, and the tech bubble popped at a height of $6.7 trillion market cap. In today's money, $6.7 trillion is the equivalent of $9.26 trillion.

- The original tech bubble and the crypto bubble are taking place under very different conditions, as shown in Table 15.2:

The original tech bubble, 1997–2000/1	The crypto bubble
It was confined mainly to just North America.	It's a global market.
It had 12 times less of a currency supply.	It has 12 times more currency in the system. This is one of the reasons why stocks and property have zoomed upwards.

There were only 272 million people in the USA and only a small percentage of those actually bought stocks.	There are between 1 and 3 billion people who *could* play with cryptos.
Social media was limited as the Internet was excruciatingly slow and Facebook had not yet been invented.	News and media are instantaneous.
Market access was limited; it was much more difficult to get set up with a financial trading account back then.	Anyone can set up a crypto account, even a shepherd in Kazakhstan on his iPhone.
There was no government intervention.	There's a large degree of government interference: Bulgaria has $3 billion worth of Bitcoin it commandeered; the FBI supposedly has 1 million Bitcoin; and other countries (including Estonia, Russia, China, Venezuela and Canada) are investing in blockchain tech.

TABLE 15.2 A comparison of the tech and crypto bubbles

Another reason why I think it will go a lot higher is because, every time there's a hard fork chain split (like Bitcoin and Bitcoin Cash), it creates market cap out of thin air that has no intrinsic value. It's much like the whole crypto market for that matter.

Yes, you read that correctly. I believe that 99 per cent of the crypto market is a meaningless hype bubble backed by nothing. It's not like Amazon where, despite its lofty $1,100-plus share price, it has epic value and substance. Right now, the whole crypto market is full of PDF white papers with grand visions and plans.

This doesn't mean that you shouldn't invest or speculate. Just remain emotionally disconnected; profit all the way up, profit all the way down, then hoover up everything to hold for good.

A note of caution

This market has rewarded and will continue to reward millions of people with poor practices such as over-leveraging, simply because of the dramatic rising tide. But when the bubble bursts, these novices won't have a clue what to do and many will retreat and hand over all their paper profits. That is why the correct information, education and training are essential.

16
Seven reasons why you should own some cryptos

If you've been paying attention, you'll know that there is a compelling case to invest in or speculate in cryptos, whether you believe cryptos have longevity or not. We are due to see one of the world's fastest-growing markets in recent history – or possibly ever.

But in case you're still sitting on the fence, here are seven simple reasons why it's essential you and your family get some exposure:

1 **This is the first major asset class to be created since 1694.**

No, that isn't a typo. The last time a major asset class like this was introduced to the world was the British government's Gilded Edge Bond in 1694. The interesting thing here is that human nature never changes. When shiny new things enter the scene, people are naturally curious and capital flows in. Basic economics dictates that when capital pours into an asset, prices rise (all things being equal) and when capital flees or is extracted from an asset, prices drop. With cryptos, capital is pouring in. At the beginning of 2017 the market cap was $17.7 billion and by the end of the year it was touching $800 billion!

2 **Almost half the people on the planet don't have access to the Internet or a bank account.**

Around 3.2 billion people are not yet online and don't have a bank account. Many large corporations are addressing this and it won't be long before big companies will be beaming free Internet to the whole of the African continent and South-East Asia, where most of this demographic live. This, combined with very cheap (under $25) smartphones, will make the early twenty-first century the New Age of Enlightenment. These may be lofty dreams, but many estimates say this will happen within the next ten years. And when it does, it's extremely probable that crypto accounts (which you can create in minutes) will be more popular than traditional bank accounts.

Changing the planet

I'm half Thai, half English, and my mum is from one of the poorest parts of Thailand. In her village running water and electricity are rare, and everyone has to fish or trade to secure a meal. But the thing I've found about many of the poorest parts of the world is that the people stuck in these areas are incredibly entrepreneurial. They have to be. So, despite 3.2 billion people living in the extremes of poverty, the majority are extremely switched on and hardworking. I really can't wait to see what this half of the planet brings to the table when they come online.

3 The crypto market cap is exploding

The year 2017 was a big one for cryptos, in both capital and the number of cryptos coming online. The market cap grew by over 4,500 per cent and, although I don't think 2018 will equal the same percentage growth, it will dwarf 2017 in actual quantities of capital pouring in. While 2017 didn't hit $1 trillion, during 2018 I expect to see multiple trillions entering this market. We are standing on the precipice of huge inflows.

Looking back at the standard bubble wave (see Chapter 14), we are now entering the media phase. The public are starting to wake up about cryptos, and Wall Street is now wading in with its myriad derivatives. The Initial Coin Offering (ICO) side market is starting to really scare venture capitalists, as many crypto projects have launched by doing an ICO and have quickly raised billions of dollars in a matter of weeks.

Another factor is the upward pressure that the introduction of crypto exchange-traded funds (ETFs) will have on the market. An ETF is a financial instrument that trades like a stock but mimics the price of the underlying asset. This is how traders can trade exotic assets like oil, gold, uranium and soybeans without actually having to take delivery of them. What is happening at the moment is that a flurry of Bitcoin and cryptocurrency ETFs are about to come online, which will allow people to play with the crypto market without actually investing in cryptos. The crucial thing to note is that with most ETFs, in order to set one up, you have to buy the underlying asset first in order to launch and sell your ETF. In simple terms, this means that, if I wanted to set up a $100-million-Bitcoin ETF, I would need to go and buy $100 million worth of Bitcoin. All of this will add positive pressure to prices.

4 **Blockchain will consume the planet just as the Internet did.**
Blockchain or distributed ledger technologies (DLTs) will continue to disrupt and streamline any and all industries they touch. I cannot stress enough that what the Internet did for communication in terms of sheer disruption/innovation, cryptos will do for money and blockchain tech will do for trust.

Every middleman business will become extinct within 10–15 years, as an efficient market has no need for 'margin slicers/flow inhibitors'. These include business brokers, estate agents and even accountants to some extent. One thing I've been saying for a while is that it won't be long before someone puts a estate agency completely online on a smart-contract-based blockchain, where users will be able to buy a house for less than £10 in fees and in less than ten minutes. There is absolutely no reason why anyone should wait months to sell their house and be fleeced to the tune of thousands, all the while being delayed by the various middlemen.

Blockchain tech will make its way into anything you can imagine, from your smart devices at home to air traffic control, automated cars, auditing, remittances, voting systems, land registries, medical records, insurance, trading and financial services.

5 **We are nowhere near 'peak bubble'.**
I've mentioned several times already that this tiny market is set to explode in terms of market cap, talent attraction, investor attraction and government regulation. This bubble is most likely to blow the previous tech bubble out of the water in terms of its size and speed.

A rough rule of thumb, with game-changing innovative tech/industries like this, is that the bubble is likely to grow to at least twice the size in half the time and also crash harder in half the time. On that basis, we should be looking at a $20 trillion market cap by the end of 2019, followed by a sharp crash spanning 9–15 months, with a 90 per cent or more decline in prices and quantity of cryptos. Whether or not it will play out like that, nobody really knows, but this is a fabulous opportunity in the short term to jump into this soon-to-be-rising tide and capitalize on the growth.

6 **It's potentially the best hedge against sovereign intervention and market pandemics.**
There are many uncertainties in the markets, but one thing it's safe to assume is that whenever a new unregulated market comes on to the scene, governments and their regulators won't be far behind to sanction and impose measures 'to protect the public from unregulated/

unruly investments'. That's the pretext they normally use to approach these things, but the objective is really to try to control it in order to collect the necessary taxes they feel are owed to the coffers. What history beautifully illustrates, to those who study it, is that, whenever a government has tried to ban, fix the price or control a certain asset, it doesn't always go to plan and, in most cases, the very asset they were coming down on ends up growing even more. This happened with gold in the early 1930s, when the USA tried to ban private ownership of gold, and you can go all the way back to the Roman Emperor Diocletian in 301 CE, who imposed the 'Edict of Maximum Prices' in an attempt to address the world's first outbreak of hyperinflation. One of the measures he imposed was a ban on selling salt above a certain amount, the infringement of which was punishable by death. This was important for him, as all soldiers were paid in salt (this is where our word 'salary' comes from). Despite this, the price of salt continued to rise.

Whatever the world's governments try to do, the complexity, flexibility, stealth and invulnerability of cryptos will make it all futile. Cryptos are like the fabled Hydra, except it has tens of thousands, if not hundreds of thousands, of heads distributed across the world.

If you really wanted to, you could completely mask all your crypto activity by using privacy coins like Spectre, which completely obfuscates all transactions, addresses, wallets and messaging using ring signatures, stealth addresses and TOR OBFS4. You don't need to know what all those terms mean but, in essence, Spectre coin offers complete privacy and using TOR OBFS4 allows undetected use of TOR in countries that block it, such as China and Iran.

Regarding market pandemics, what you'll find is that when a market collapses, as the stock market did in 1987, 2001 and 2008, investors flee to areas of perceived 'safe-haven' such as gold and silver bullion, land, the US dollar, the Japanese yen and cash in general. No one can say for certain, but I believe cryptos will be added to this basket of safe havens. The crypto market isn't battle-tested yet; we have seen it only in the post-2009 economic boom. What will be fascinating is what happens to cryptos during the next stock market crash. If I were to put money on it (which I am), I'd say cryptos will do well.

According to Forbes at the end of 2017 there were 2,043 billionaires, and according to Credit Suisse there were 35 million millionaires. This doesn't account for all the 'black money' people in the background, so these figures are rather conservative. Credit Suisse stated that the richest 1 per cent now owns 50 per cent of the world's wealth. That's a total combined wealth of $280 trillion. If these people just allocated 3 per cent of this wealth to the crypto market, we would see $8.4 trillion flooding the market and booming prices. I believe that this is already starting to happen, which is why we saw some irregular inflows and outflows of market cap running up towards the end of 2017. This is an overt 'tell' that the Big Money is pulling the market back down while loading up more for themselves.

7 This is the biggest bubble and 'greater fool's game' ever.

A great stock tip

There's a classic tale in the investment world about Joseph P. Kennedy, the father of President John F. Kennedy. Around 1929 Joseph stopped for a shoeshine on his way to work and, while chatting, the shoeshine said something along the lines of 'Sir, I've got a great stock tip for you!' Joe, an accomplished investor, knew that, if the general public was rushing into an asset, the top was in and it was time to get out. On the back of this, Joseph sold all his stocks and dodged the 1929 Crash beautifully, which helped him become one of the richest men in the USA during the Great Depression.

What's happening now is a huge short-term bubble, and it's the public wading in that will boom and pop it. This was originally a reason I kept cryptos at arm's length, but I decided to open my mind and hunt for the opportunity. If I'm correct and we do see all this capital and interest flooding the market and the crypto market cap hits $10 trillion or more before it starts popping, this presents us with the three biggest ever profit-making opportunities, as outlined in Chapter 14:

- Exponential growth
- Shorting it
- A slow rally.

That's why I'm so passionate that everyone needs some exposure to this. To miss out on these opportunities is simply sacrilegious. You will never in your lifetime see another net-worth leapfrogging event like this, ever. The next chapter explains the three biggest opportunities …

17

The three biggest opportunities of your lifetime – and how to capitalize on them

As described in Chapter 16, the three biggest opportunities to capitalize on in your lifetime are exponential growth, shorting it and a slow rally. Opportunity 1 (growth) is about being super-aggressive in your acquisition of cryptos; Opportunity 2 is about being very aggressive (shorting it); and Opportunity 3 (a slow rally) is more of a 'set-and-forget' strategy. Here is how to capitalize on them.

Opportunity 1 – exponential growth

The first opportunity is the potential crazy blow-off top bubble that effectively started forming at the beginning of 2017 and may pop around 2019/20.

The public hasn't cottoned on yet, but they always do the wrong thing at the wrong time. It's simply a matter of time before people start wading in with their uninformed actions. This is a 'greater fool's game': we get in now, profit immensely during the vertical run-up the public and institutional money will cause, and exit the market and take profits off the table around the $10 trillion market cap level. This is where I'll take 80–90 per cent of my profits off the table back into Fiat, where I'll divest back into businesses and land.

As keen as I am on this market, I'm not deluded. I am well aware that 99 per cent of this market is fuelled by nonsense, 'fake news', hype, future hopes and greed. I'm simply capitalizing on human nature and converting my profits from this hype market back into real, tangible assets where you can store real long-lasting generational wealth.

The reason I'm not taking 100 per cent of profits off the table is because I know my own flaws. In my investing career I am normally 100 per cent on the money, but nearly always early. This is mainly because I get right down into the nitty-gritty of an asset at a deep level, long before most people cotton on, so my investing radar is very sensitive to movements which leave me entering or exiting a big move slightly early. Therefore the 10–20 per cent I'll leave in cryptos is just in case it runs all the way up to $20 trillion, $30 trillion or $50 trillion before popping.

Opportunity 2 – shorting it

When it becomes obvious that the market is going to crash, this is when I'll extract nearly all profits. No matter how solid you think your beloved crypto is, it will crumble in price during this blow-off top period. It's exactly the same with Microsoft, Amazon and Apple. Even these three giants lost vast amounts of wealth as a result of falling share prices back in the tech bubble pop.

The opportunity here, which the vast majority of people will never spot, is the 'shorting' opportunity. Most people think you can make money only when a market is going up. Wrong. You can make money in up, down and sideways-moving markets, but you can make the most amount of money in the shortest possible time in crashing markets. Falling markets, you see, move 3.3 times faster than rising markets. But crashing markets fall at least ten times faster. This is why there's a trading saying that you take the stairs to the top of the building and then the elevator down.

In a nutshell, for the uninitiated, traders can profit from falling markets just as easily as rising ones. All you do is effectively trade/bet on the movement of the asset, whether it's going up or down. It's just like going to the races and betting on a horse to win or lose. You don't own the horse or the jockey; you're simply betting on the movement and result of the horse.

Trading an asset in the hope that the price will rise is called 'going long', while trading an asset in the hope that it will go down is called 'going short'.

From the peak of the inevitable crypto pop, I'm expecting it to fall at the very least 80 per cent in market cap and prices. I will short it until we hit those lows, but, in terms of what money/profits I'll leave in, I don't know what percentage of my portfolio it will be.

Once the market has lost around 80 per cent of its value, we enter Opportunity 3.

Opportunity 3 – a slow rally

This is the chilled-out part of the plan. The reason Opportunity 3 is a considerably longer phase is because, after the crash, cryptos will eventually segue into the established phase, which means the ridiculous volatility will cease, pension funds and other risk-averse Big Money will start to treat it as a legitimate asset class just like stocks and bonds, and it will no doubt be a regulated market. On the whole, ten years on from the pop, the crypto market will just seem like a sensible asset class.

In essence, I will adopt Warren Buffett's style of investing. After the pop I will simply hoover up all the 'blue chip' solid cryptos that have survived the fall, buy up any promising ones and never sell. Opportunity 3 is simply catching the immense growth and maturity of the crypto market as it makes its way to consuming large chunks of the stock and bond markets and also eating the whole foreign exchange market.

Just as Warren Buffett learned from his mentor Benjamin Graham that 'You need to be fearful when others are greedy and be greedy when others are fearful', you need to buy when there is blood on the streets.

18
The future effect of cryptos on business and the economy

If you were a switched-on cookie back in the mid-1990s, you would have no doubt seen the raw future potential of the Internet and what it might do for the world. You would have predicted how it would revolutionize communication and make the world a smaller and more connected place. But it would have been impossible to forecast just how prolific the Internet would become.

Now, more than 20 years later, we can see how the Internet has infiltrated every single aspect of life and all industries. Most businesses would grind to a halt without it. It's simply the linchpin of the modern world.

The more I dive down into this subject, I can't help but think that in 20 years' time we'll have a similar situation with blockchain. We won't be able to function coherently without DLTs (distributed ledger technologies), aka blockchain tech, and its future improvements. DLTs will be woven into the fabric of pretty much everything, just like the Internet, which is why it's crucial that we all play both the short-term and the long-term game.

We need quick, aggressive action to capitalize on the pure hype and stupidity of this short-term bubble and then more sustainable approaches 'post-pop', like setting up businesses around DLTs. The possibilities are endless. It won't be long before businesses are connected via multiple DAPPS (decentralized applications) to some sort of smart contract-based blockchain. This would totally automate many time-consuming things such as bookkeeping and accounting.

Just think about it for a second. Your business finances will be connected to a crypto wallet and the moment a client pays you, the crypto funds land in your wallet. The wallet is connected to a blockchain via a DAPP, which automatically records the transaction, and the taxes are automatically pinged to a 'tax wallet' for when it's time to pay your relevant taxes (which it will do automatically). As this will all be on a blockchain that is immutable once inputted, there won't be any need to file end-of-year tax returns or accounts or VAT returns because everything will be squared away as you go. There'll be no more creative accounts, no more rushing around at the end of the year and no more filling forms trying to raise funding, only for a bank or lending firm to reject your application.

All you will need to do is grant whoever you're trying to borrow from a special view-only key to your finance block-chain and they'll instantly see how creditworthy you are and the funds can be in your wallet in seconds.

This is just a tiny example of what the future is likely to hold. What other changes can we expect in the next decade or so?

The business sector

- **Middlemen businesses will become redundant or extinct.**
  This will happen within about 15 years, when around 99 per cent of these businesses, like estate agents, business brokers, banks, and accountants and bookkeepers, will cease to exist in their current form.

- **Land registries will be on a blockchain.**
  In many developing countries people may live in their home for years or spend their life saving up to buy their plot of land, only for corrupt politicians and police to turf them out. In these tragic instances, the victims are utterly power-less. If the deeds were on a blockchain, though, it could not happen. This is a fantastic, empowering use of blockchain tech, which I fervently hope is implemented soon.

- **Medical records will be on a blockchain.**
  If you've ever moved to a new location, you'll know that transferring medical records is an absolute chore. There is so much inefficiency around it but it can easily be fixed. If everyone's medical records were on a blockchain, you would have full control of your own records. You could simply issue whatever surgery you go to with a special key to access your records. A crypto called Patientory is doing just this. You could take this one step further and connect your fingerprint to your medical records, so if you were involved in an accident on holiday, they could just scan your fingerprint and know your blood type, allergies and special notes. This could potentially save lives.

- **There will be proper peer-to-peer (P2P) lending.**
  The P2P lending we have at the moment is definitely not proper P2P. If I were to raise funding for my business through one of the crowd-funding sites like Funding Circle, Crowd Cube or Kickstarter, people would have to send money from their bank account to the website bank account and then, upon successful completion of the raise, the website would take around 5 per cent commission. In this convoluted process there are three middlemen: the two bank accounts and the crowd-funding company. In five years all these middlemen lending platforms will either die out or pivot into decentralized lending exchanges. This way, if your business wants to raise funding, you can do it via a similar-looking website/platform, but with all the contributions going directly into your own crypto wallet with some sort of smart contract to look after the repayments. This, of course, would be

the same for personal finance funding. Long story short, donations or loans will go directly from peer to peer without any middlemen.

- **You'll be able to access vast data storage at a fraction of the current price.**

Right now in the storage sector, Google Drive and Dropbox are the big boys. However, even today data storage is expensive and not that secure. In addition, *you do not own your data – these companies do.* With crypto/ blockchain tech, these major players are under a real threat of being made redundant unless they, too, pivot and copy the new crypto storage way, where you upload your data to the network, it's shredded into tiny chunks and dispersed throughout the network all over the globe. Each computer in the network will receive only a tiny part of the data and can never see or reconstitute it back up; it's as though they've received a slice of a shredded document.

When *you* want to access your data, you have a private key, which is the only thing that can mesh it all back together again. You have full control and ownership of your data for a fraction of current prices. The clever part about the whole system is the network contributors – in other words, you and me. When you go to bed at night you can just leave your computer connected to the network and it will use a small portion of unused hard drive, in return for which you are rewarded with tokens/coins from that network. Check out Siacoin and Maidsafe, mentioned in Chapter 10. You can earn Siacoins just by connecting your computer to the network and it doesn't slow your computer down.

- **You'll be able to rent supercomputer time at a fraction of the current price.**
  I also mentioned distributed computing in Chapter 10. To recap, if you were a scientist or in the business of crunching lots of data and wanted to rent some time on a supercomputer, it would cost anywhere from $1,000 to $10,000 per hour depending on how much computing power you needed. Using an almost identical model to data storage, you can have vast computing power at your fingertips for pennies. What happens is that people all over the world connect their computers to the network, the network uses a small portion of unused RAM on each computer and the network benefits from huge amounts of power depending on how many contributors there are. Everyone is paid in that network's token. Users simply log into the network and pay for computer power at a fraction of the current cost. It's a beautiful use of crypto tech.

- **Hundreds of mini stock markets will be created.**
  Right now in the UK there are three main stock markets that most of us are familiar with: the FTSE 100, the FTSE 250 and the AIM (penny stock) market. Of course there are more, but if you go back 60 years there were literally dozens and dozens of stock markets and I believe that over the next ten years we will see a many mini stock markets coming online using blockchain/crypto tech similar to P2P lending.

  As things stand, if a company wants to raise capital but doesn't want to go down the debt route, it's a chore with a lot of luck mixed in. Some businesses stumble across a well-suited angel investor but most don't. They just continually struggle and are forced to bootstrap (grow organically) their way to success.

Go Norwich!

I'm from a small British city called Norwich and, despite its being a fine city, it is somewhat lacking in local business support. Norwich would be a prime candidate to have its own stock market, where local micro-businesses could muster direct investment. Smart investors could use these local stock markets to good effect. If, say, a new train route or motorway or something good was being planned to happen in or near the town, one could simply invest in a Norwich business tracker fund or even invest in the businesses that would have a dramatic uptick in growth as a result of new developments.

The economy

- **Political voting will be online and on a blockchain.**
  I'm sure many would agree with me when I say that our current voting system is a diabolical shambles. Many people don't trust it and, even in a world of interconnectivity, we still can't vote online, which means that many people don't bother to vote at all. If a country created a completely decentralized, open-source, public blockchain for voting, it would be a game-changer. It would be completely transparent and immutable; the public would trust it and, if you were also able to vote from your mobile, voter turnout would be unprecedented. This would be especially helpful in unstable and corrupt countries that are pretty much gangster run and dominated.

- **National currencies will eventually be 'cryptofied'.**
  A while ago I coined the terms 'cryptofied' and 'sovereign cryptofication' (see the box below), to refer to a process whereby a country would move from its existing currency to a 'cryptofied' version of its currency. It hasn't happened yet but it will slowly happen over the next 20 years or so. In fact, it's looking increasingly probable that Venezuela will do so in the near future. Venezuela is already set to experience a major crisis with ravaging hyperinflation. It's already struggling with its four-digit inflation. What is likely to happen is that, in the not-too-distant future, the country will be so financially desperate that it will have to default on all its debts and simply adopt a crypto like Bitcoin or something similar as its new de facto sovereign currency. Either that, or the country will just issue its own crypto (for free) and force it upon its people, thereby putting off a difficult decision.

  In more developed countries the process will be more gradual, most likely spanning a decade. In this way, the population will just grow to accept it ... in much the same way as contactless technology has just crept into bank cards seemingly out of nowhere and we all just use it now without really thinking.

Sovereign cryptofication

Let's take the UK as an example of what is likely to happen. It will introduce its own national cryptocurrency called the e-pound, which will run alongside the existing pound sterling. What will give this new crypto instant value overnight is that the UK Government will decree that it's fully legitimate and that you can pay your taxes with it. That's the key part here. They will make it very easy to use and, before you know it, every shop in the UK will accept e-pounds and may even use existing financial infrastructure to facilitate this. It will be like having your e-pound wallet connected to a debit card with contactless. You'll just continue life as usual.

What they'll do then is overtly go to war against cash. They'll get rid of the £50 note, then the £20 note, and then the rest. People may not think it's a big deal, but it is. And it has insidious and sinister ramifications down the line. You see, if you remove the £50 note from circulation, you effectively halve the UK currency supply. You won't notice it, though, as they will probably 'print/issue' an equivalent amount of e-pounds.

They will justify this war on cash under the banner that the country is progressing to a completely cashless society in order to stamp out tax evasion, money laundering and cash-in-hand jobs. This may seem logical and it will no doubt be dressed up in some nice advertisements endorsed by celebrities, but it's actually a trap.

That's because, in a completely cashless society with a sovereign crypto, there will be no privacy. The Government will know exactly what you earn, where you earn it and what you do with it. They can tax you whenever they want and, more importantly, they will have the power to go to negative interest rates and you won't be able to do a thing about it. That's the real goal. Think about it. If everyone has moved over to the e-pound and the Government/Bank of England says 'Sorry, times are tough, interest rates are now minus 1 per cent …' you will lose money every year. If you have £10,000 in your savings, next year you'll have £9,900. Imagine the income negative rates would generate for the Government across the 70 million people in the UK? It would be tens of billions per year.

19
Why blockchain is not the
future of blockchain

As you know by now, the core underlying tech on which cryptos are built is blockchain tech. Like a fancy online spreadsheet visible and accessible to all, it's a digital record of all prior transactions spread across the world that are used to verify the ownership and validity of transactions. Originally, blockchains were designed to be 'permission-less' (public), with no one able to control or manipulate them. It sounds dreamy and idealistic doesn't it? 'In maths we trust', as they say. In reality, a blockchain that uses the Proof of Work 'mining systems' that power most cryptos is quickly becoming archaic. It's too energy guzzling, has scalability issues and is inefficient by design because the whole system is *designed to be slow* as a security feature. If a system like this were too fast, it could result in runaway chains of incorrect and unconfirmed blocks.

If Generation 1 blockchain were a car, it would be steampowered. It was a massive breakthrough, but was not exactly feasible or sustainable. That's is why I always mutter under my breath when I hear someone say that blockchain is the future. It's really not: the *concept* of blockchain, that is, distributed ledger technologies, yes; blockchain … no.

From Generation 1 to Generation 4

What makes this sector fascinating is that we are already playing with Generation-3-type blockchains.

First-generation cryptos/blockchains ran from 2009 to 2016, and from 2016 to 2017 we've jumped two generations of tech development. Generation 2 saw the introduction of smart contract-based blockchains made famous by the Ethereum network. Generation-3-type blockchains feature multi-layered delegated Proof of Stake (as showcased by Cardano), DLTs like

Tangle used by IOTA, Hyperledger developed by IBM, Block Lattice used by Nano, and also the Hashgraph.

Tangle, Hyperledger, Block Lattice and Hashgraph could even be considered fourth-generation DLTs. If traditional blockchains are the steam car, Tangle, Hyperledger, Block Lattice and Hashgraph are fighter jets. Not only are they able to achieve millions, if not billions, of transactions per second (which is crucial for a globally scaled, everyday-use micro-transactions crypto), but they also have infinite scale.

Nearly all cryptos face scaling issues. They're fine at the moment while there are limited users in the crypto space, but when it goes mainstream there are going to be problems. Put it this way: if there were four people around a table with a big pizza, everyone would get a good slice. But if 50 people suddenly walked in and you had to equally share that same pizza, there would be queues and the slices would be tiny! These fourth-generation DLTs actually improve the more users they have. It's like all new users walking into the room with their own pizza.

A new benchmark has been set with new cryptos like Nano (formerly Rai Blocks), as it now does instant transactions with zero fees and with infinite scalability. Any crypto coming online that doesn't meet this minimum benchmark is a step backwards. With the bubble pop rapidly nearing, I'm becoming increasingly picky with my crypto acquisitions.

One development that could be interesting is the future of the International Monetary Fund's Special Drawing Right (SDR). Put simply, the Bank of England can print pounds, the European Central Bank can print euros and the Federal Reserve can print dollars. The central banks of the world control, monitor and maintain their respective currency supplies and interest rates. That's their job.

The IMF sits above the central banks and can print SDRs – another Fiat currency. SDRs are basically 'world money', and most countries in the world have to maintain a certain quota of SDRs. Whenever a country needs a big bail-out, it is often with SDRs, the only form of world money other than gold.

Cryptos are accelerating the world into a cashless society and also perhaps a one-world currency, and what's happening right now is that the IMF is working on a permissioned 'private' system for the SDR, which could potentially use IBM's Hyperledger. By converting the SDR into a cryptocurrency that uses a fast and scalable DLT like Hyperledger, it would enable inter-bank and inter-country transactions like bilateral trade surpluses to be instant and potentially free. This would save governments and the banking system billions of dollars per year.

This Hyperledger SDR would be issued to all 189 members of the IMF and would quickly become the new global reserve currency, thereby dealing a massive blow to the US dollar and its tyrannical petrodollar system. It won't happen overnight but it's going to be fascinating watching this happen.

20

Scams, scams and MLMs – and how to detect and avoid them

This is probably the most important chapter of the book. I feel it's my duty to shine a 1,000-watt spotlight on this topic because many people are being cheated and they don't even know it. The only thing I respect about these scams is their marketing department.

In this chapter I will cover the biggest cons in the crypto space to help you spot when you are being swindled. First, though, I'm going to describe the 'scam yardstick' so that you are aware of the different types of scheme out there.

Ponzi schemes

Bernie Madoff is synonymous with the phrase Ponzi scheme; he's even more famous than Charles Ponzi himself, after whom the scheme was named. Over the space of 25 years, Bernie Madoff swindled around $65 billion out of the US economy. He's now serving 150 years in prison.

The concept of a Ponzi is rather simple:

1 You 'invest' £1,000 in a company/scheme that promises a high and consistent return, something like a 10 per cent return over six months. Let's say your repayment date is in June, when you'll be '£100 up'.

2 This company then gets another person to 'invest'. However, the company is not actually investing in anything; it's just using the new money coming in to pay off the first victim.

3 The company now has two victims to which it owes money. So what does it do? Yes, you guessed it, it goes out and finds another victim and uses that new money to pay the existing victims.

4 Then it's a case of repeating the process until there is no one left to 'recruit'. At this point, it's game over. Everyone loses money apart from the operators, who were making a fortune throughout the whole operation. Bernie Madoff became a multi-billionaire as a result.

There are a few things in motion here that are crucial to understand. When the scheme/company is good at getting new blood in, the scheme seems absolutely fantastic to the victims involved, because they think they are making silly ROI by doing nothing. And whenever they check their accounts, it certainly looks as if they're in profit.

That's one reason why a lot of Ponzi victims are defensive and loyal: they *think* they're in profit (from doing nothing). In reality, in most cases, if they were to try to extract and cash in on their new 'profits' they wouldn't be able to. There are many cases out there where victims have tried to pull their money out of a Ponzi, only to be hard-sold a new and even better product to invest in – or the cash withdrawal process is so laboured that people don't bother with it.

Crypto MLMs

An MLM is a multi-level marketing scheme or a network-marketing scheme, or even a pyramid-selling scheme in some cases. Some MLMs are actually sound companies that have good products and great customer service and that look after their 'distributers'. But most of them are not. You also need to remember that decentralization and disintermediation of industries are the whole *raison d'être* of cryptos. It's totally incongruous for *any* crypto MLM to exist.

I once met a distributer from a crypto MLM who was trying to sell me Bitcoin at a premium. Bitcoin at the time was around $6,000 and he was trying to sell it to me for $7,000, with the justification that he would be my point of contact and that this transaction would also come with a comprehensive PDF about cryptos, along with a few videos. I quickly explained that there was no way that I would ever pay a 16.7 per cent premium on Bitcoin when I could log into any one of my numerous exchanges and buy it at spot price. If I'd bought ten Bitcoin from him, he would have got $10,000 of commission for a PDF.

One of the quickest and easiest ways to spot an MLM is by the affiliate schemes they have in place with their distributers/introducers. If Alan at the top introduced Bob into the company/scheme/product, then Alan would get a commission. But if Bob then introduced Carla, Alan would still get a commission as well as Bob, as Alan is the 'upline'. And if Carla then introduced Dave, then Carla, Bob and Alan would all get commissions. In some MLMs this goes up to ten levels deep! No wonder there is often such a hefty premium on whatever product they're selling: it's because all those people have to be paid.

Crypto lending schemes

These are just standard Ponzi schemes tarted up in a new dress. Like Ponzis, they rely on 'new blood' but because they have a 'lending facility' it completely obfuscates the whole scam. Basically, users can 'borrow' money from other lenders, who then get a nice interest from their loan and the borrowers can then loan that money to others. While all this is happening and everyone is borrowing and lending from each other, no actual money or funds are being moved, as they are only 'paper profits' in the first place. The company makes money from the annual fees it charges and a slice of every debt within their system.

Introducing Broker (IB) churn

This isn't a big scam in the crypto world yet, but I guarantee it will be. How am I so sure? I've been trading currencies for 13 years now and IB churn scams are, even today, still rife here in the foreign exchange (FX) market. It's just a matter of time before it spills over into the crypto domain. So what is it?

An introducing broker (IB) agreement is simply an agreement that a trading broker/exchange gives to an introducer. Once the introducer has introduced a trader to their exchange, the introducer gets a cut of the trading spread/commission every time that trader places a trade. This might not sound too alarming until you see how corrupt the retail FX market has become. There are so many conflicts of interest that the punter (the average retail trader – in other words, you and me) is getting slaughtered.

Let's say you're going to trade the euro against the dollar – otherwise known as 'eurodollar'. The price may be 1.2510/1.2512. As you can see, there is a difference between those two prices, which is called the spread. In this case, it's a spread of two 'pips'. Now let's say a trader places a trade on eurodollar at £10 per pip. What this basically means is that, for every pip the market goes up, the trader makes £10. So if he/she places a buy trade at 1.2512 and it goes up to 1.2522, the market has gone up ten pips, which means he/she will have made £100. Nice and simple.

But here's the thing: regardless of what the trader does, he/she will always be paying the spread. So with a two-pip spread at £10 per pip, the broker will make £20 from that trade regardless of whether the trader wins or loses the trade. Looking at the bigger picture, the average retail trader uses a style of trading called day trading, which is where you spend three to eight hours a day chained to your charts and screens and you place numerous trades per day. It's a horrible way of life and incredibly stressful. The average retail trader places ten trades per day at an average position size of £10 per pip, so with an average spread of two pips that means:

- ten trades per day x 2-pip spread x £10 per pip = £200 in commissions to the broker per day.
- an average of five days' trading per week = £1,000 per week = £4,000 in commissions per month!

But here is the crazy bit. The average introducer kickback with these IB agreements is 40 per cent. So, in this scenario, the introducer would make £1,600 per month from this day trader until the trader blows his/her account. This is why there is a very good reason for the saying that '90 per cent of traders lose 90 per cent of their capital in the first 90 days'.

As these introducer kickbacks are so juicy, what happens is that you get a sea of trading educators selling expensive day trading courses that teach the general public how to place as many trades as possible – because for every trade they place, the trading educator gets a kickback. Even if the trading educator preys on the financially inadequate and the introducing kickbacks are, say, a quarter of the example above, all he/she needs to do is maintain at least 100 trading students trading at any point in time and that's a healthy £40,000-per-month business. By the end of 2018 I'm sure we'll start seeing a wave of marketers/inexperienced crypto trading educators selling day trading courses.

Crypto trading bots

Don't bother trying to create or buy into a crypto trading bot. You won't win – unless you have millions to plough into a high-frequency trading machine-learning algorithmic bot. Also, if you ever buy into a super-secret black box trading bot, guess what? The proprietor will have an IB agreement with the broker that the bot uses. So no doubt the bot will be deploying high-frequency day trades to churn out those commissions.

High-yielding constant investment schemes

HYCIS are something you should always be wary of in all financial markets. Here's a bona fide fact: markets are *not* consistent. Therefore you simply cannot have a scheme that pays out consistent monthly returns. It's mathematically impossible for a HYCIS to last in the long run, so run away the moment you hear or see of any scheme that gives out 1 per cent per month or a guaranteed 15 per cent per year.

I once saw a scam that said it paid out a guaranteed 6 per cent per month. Just think about that for a moment. If you started with £1,000, at 6 per cent per month, you'd have £2,012.19 at the end of Year 1 and £32,987.69 after five years. It may sound incredibly attractive, but, via the markets, it's not going to happen. If you want 70 per cent plus ROI per year, the only feasible way is to set up, run and grow your own business. And even that comes with a truck-load of risk and sweat, toil and tears over the years.

> Long story short, you can't get easy profits by doing nothing!

Cash-grabbing forks

You now know from a previous chapter that whenever there is a chain split, if you own the original currency during the snapshot, you will be credited with an equal amount of coins with the new forked crypto.

If you'd owned five BTC during its first chain-splitting hard fork, then you also got five BCH. It was a sort of Bitcoin quantitative easing. Everyone with the knowledge and know-how jumped on the bandwagon and created a number of different Bitcoin chain splits as a form of a cash grab. When the new forked crypto is listed on an exchange, they dump it. There is now a sea of bad Bitcoin forks like Bitcoin Gold, X, Platinum, Diamond, Oil, World, Stake, Faith, Cash Plus, Silver, Pizza, God, Super Bitcoin and many more on the upcoming fork list.

Beware also of cryptos that effectively steal the name of an existing established crypto. There was a recent announcement that there would be a Litecoin hard fork and that the new crypto would be called Litecoin Cash. Charlie Lee (the founder of Litecoin) quickly came out on Twitter saying that it had nothing to do with Litecoin and that it was definitely a cash-grabbing scam.

Fake wallets

When googling to find the official wallet of a coin, you need to be on red alert for scams because there are myriad phishing or cloned websites that look like the official website. If you're not careful, you could download a wallet that is actually a virus that will not only scour your computer for your passwords and private keys, but give the scammer total control of your cryptos when you send them to the fake wallet.

If a crypto doesn't have a wallet to download from their official website, make sure to look on the official github thread for that crypto. The official updated wallet will be there.

Mining pitfalls

Mining Bitcoin and other cryptos has been a rewarding activity for many years now. It appeals to the laziness within all of us, as you can just buy a crypto mining rig, set it all up and have it producing 'money' 24/7. Who doesn't want a money machine? But the gravy train we have seen from 2010 to 2017 is ending. Over the next few years the difficulty of mining will increase dramatically as a result of the global hashrate increasing, especially in Bitcoin.

In addition, the reward a miner gets will diminish over the next few years, not just with Bitcoin where the block reward halves in May 2020, but also for many different Proof of Work coins. With Bitcoin's block reward halving to 6.25 BTC, the price of BTC really needs to increase to a point where it's still economically feasible to mine it.

Miners will say something along the lines of, 'But my mining rig has a software that automatically scans the market and mines the most profitable coin in real time. And over the next year, hundreds of Proof of Work coins are coming online.' This may well be true, but what a lot of miners don't understand is that there is a growing wave of anti-PoW feeling due to the energy consumption issue, so it wouldn't surprise me if there were a global ban on mining rigs that aren't powered by renewable energy sources.

I personally hope this law is put in place because it would spark a massive solar tech drive, especially as Bitcoin is set to consume more energy per year than Japan by 2023.

Regarding the other coins to mine, yes, there will be hundreds of other coins, but, as with anything, the focus should be on quality rather than quantity. Since 99 per cent of cryptos won't last or survive the bubble pop, if you're mining one of the many 'shitcoins' out there it's a waste of time. When mining, you want to be mining a coin that appreciates in price. Mining a dying coin is a futile exercise.

Zero-utility cryptos

This one may seem like common sense, but it's not so common. I often get questions like, 'Siam, what are your thoughts about [insert any bogus coin]?' I then have a look at it and realize that there is zero real-world use for this crypto — as in, there is literally no use for it. Yes, you could ping it directly to others, so it's a form of value transfer but, with most cryptos like this, their network effect or network value is negligible because hardly anyone is using it.

The sad fact is that over 95 per cent of cryptos fall into this category, as most are useless with zero real-world utility. Even for value transfer cryptos (currency), now that the benchmark has been set by NANO with instant transactions, zero fees and infinite scalability, if a new crypto comes on to the market and doesn't at least match those features then they should just give up. When the inevitable crypto bloodbath comes and 90 per cent of market cap, cryptos and prices drop, only the hardy blue-chip cryptos will survive. It's much like how Amazon, Microsoft, Apple and IBM survived the tech bubble pop.

ICOs

This is going to be controversial because there has been a big buzz about investing in ICOs (initial coin offerings). In order to understand ICOs, let's take a step back and look at IPOs (initial public offerings).

An IPO is when a private company launches itself on to a stock market. When it does this it has to sell at least 25 per cent of its stock to the public. Once it's launched on a market, the company will have a 'ticker', normally a three- or four-letter abbreviation for the stock. For example, Vodafone is VOD, Tesla is TSLA and Amazon is AMZN. It's the same for cryptos. For instance, Basic Attention Token's ticker is BAT and Humaniq's is HMQ. IPOs have been a very lucrative industry for decades now and it's normally a way for the major shareholders of a company to realize great wealth in a very short time. When Mark Zuckerberg IPO'd Facebook, he went from rich to absurdly rich straight away, with his net worth jumping to $19.1 billion on the day of listing. It was the same for Evan Spiegel when he IPO'd Snapchat; his net worth ballooned to $636.6 million.

An ICO is basically when someone, or a group, launches a brand-new crypto to the world. They effectively launch a bunch of code and raise millions in minutes due to the manic buzz. Here is a list of some of the fastest and biggest ICOs from 2017:

- Humaniq: $1.5 million raised in 60 minutes
- Modum.io: $4.2 million raised in 10 minutes

- Firstblood: $6 million raised in few minutes
- Golem: $8.6 million in 29 minutes
- Qtum: $10 million raised in 90 minutes
- Blockchain Capital: $10 million raised in six hours
- Gnosis: $12 million raised in ten minutes
- Aragon: $25 million in 15 minutes
- Basic Attention Token: $35 million raised in 30 seconds
- Bancor: $152 million raised in three hours.

This is just a short list, but these are astonishing statistics and it's obvious why people are so excited about ICOs.

But this is where the danger lies. The moment you become excited on the markets, you're setting yourself up for inevitable pain. The amateur dabbler loves to think that he/she is getting in on something early. We all do. But with ICOs, you're almost never going to be in properly early. Do you really think all those cryptos launched their ICOs and the public just piled in? No; all the deals are pre-arranged.

I do a bit of pre-IPO investing and I know first hand how lucrative being a seed/pre-IPO investor can be. With the four IPOs I've gone into at the seed/pre-sale round, I get 100 per cent ROI contractually agreed. And it's the same with ICOs.

You often get a seed round, a pre-sale round and a public sale round. The founders, their friends and trusted investors get in on the seed round with 50–100 per cent bonuses. The seed round is there to raise a relatively small amount, like $100 k to $2 million, so it can finance the whole set-up and organization and time-cost of doing an ICO. The pre-sale round is normally offered to sophisticated/accredited investors who get a 20–40 per cent bonus and then the public are offered something like a 10–20 per cent bonus.

But here's the thing: on listing day the crypto fails upon listing on the live markets. Why is that? It's because the seed/pre-sale investors just dump their cryptos because they are suddenly liquid or they just take their original investment out and leave the 'free tokens' they now have to hold. At least 70 per cent of ICOs crash 20–80 per cent within the first month of being listed.

Here are my two top tips for investing in ICOs:

1 Don't. Just don't.
2 See the first tip.

Here are the three main reasons not to invest in ICOs:

1 At least 70 per cent of ICOs crash in price within the first month.
2 You have no idea which exchange the crypto will be listed on. If it's a bad exchange, you are exposing your capital in a crypto that may never take off. You will then be praying that a bigger exchange like Binance lists it.
3 You're losing out big time on opportunity cost! This is the most important point. Most ICOs run between three and 12 months. If you hand over your Ether and have to wait six months, for example, you're simply giving all your potential appreciation gain (PAG) to the crypto. This happened to me in May 2017. I invested $1,000/10 Ether into an ICO with Ether at $10. By the time the ICO launched, Ether was over $300! The crypto got *all* of my PAG and the crypto then failed upon listing. I lost out on $3,000 worth of Ether gain, and then again when the crypto lost 40 per cent in its opening week.

If you're keen to invest in an ICO because you genuinely believe in it, I would highly recommend that you sit on your hands and do nothing. Wait until it launches. Watch it crash and then buy in once it's halved in price. That way you keep your PAG and you'll then have a better result when you do eventually go in.

21
Wallets, exchanges and the buy/sell process

I could bore you to death with all the different ways you could go about protecting your cryptos, from beefing up your home security to changing your router settings, but there is one major thing you can do right now which won't cost you a thing. That's 'social security' – as in, simply don't tell anyone that you're in cryptos. If people don't know you have cryptos, they won't come sniffing around.

For the people around you that do know you have cryptos, just play it down. Just say you're dabbling and have a few hundred pounds or dollars in it for a laugh.

I say this because there has been a spate of crypto-related heists, and a loose friend of mine was recently held at gunpoint in his own home for his cryptos. I'm raising a young family and am well aware that I now have a target on my back for online/offline hackers so I've had to massively beef up my personal home security. I have everything: CCTV, panic rooms, quick-response systems and other home defence measures. It's not ideal but it's too late to change my public crypto status now!

There are various ways of protecting your cryptos, including wallets.

Wallets

The easiest way to get your head around wallets is to think of them in terms of your personal bank account. If you do that, things become much clearer. With your bank account you basically have three things to know: your sort code, your account number and your PIN. The sort and account number identify the name of the bank and where your account is, and the PIN is the electronic key that grants you access to your funds. It's pretty straightforward.

It's actually even simpler with crypto wallets as you only need to know two things: the public address and the private key. The public address is simply the equivalent of your bank account number and your private key is the equivalent of your PIN. That's it, although it is a bit harder to memorize your crypto wallet credentials, as your public address will be 25–36 characters and your private key can be up to 50 characters or, in some cases, 20 different words in a set order.

An added benefit of crypto wallets is that you can set one up in under 30 seconds with no documents. Try setting up a bank account in that time. It's impossible. I recently opened an additional business bank account so I could have a separate 'investment pot' for one of my businesses and, despite the bank having all my details, it still took 45 minutes on the phone! This is another reason why the banking sector is going to fail and cryptos will prevail, because when the 'unbanked' finally become 'banked' it will be with a crypto account, not a typical bank account.

The vast majority of the population trusts banks enough to look after their capital. When you get paid into your account, you don't often worry about it being hacked. But in the crypto world, personal data security is a topic you will become rapidly familiar with the more crypto wealth you amass. Necessity is a great teacher. Because you're now storing and protecting your own wealth, you need to understand that not all wallets are the same.

Wallets come in various forms, but there are generally two types: a hot wallet and a cold wallet.

Hot wallets

Hot wallets are easy and convenient to use, but not as safe as they could be. Common hot wallets are 'web wallets' where you just create an online account with a wallet provider of some sort.

Cold wallets

Cold wallets are the safest and the best way to store your cryptos. You dramatically minimize the odds of being hacked with a cold wallet, although with that extra safety you do lose convenience. It can take an extra few minutes to get your cryptos back on to an exchange to sell compared to a hot wallet, but that's a small price to pay. If you're doing things properly on the crypto market, you shouldn't really be that pushed for time.

One of the best tips I give to new aspiring traders is that the best risk-mitigation weapon they can deploy is to just sit on their hands and do nothing. Just wait an extra day. Most of the time this delay saves people thousands. The extra rigmarole and time of getting your cryptos out of cold storage may sometimes be 'too much of an effort' and end up saving you money by preventing you from making rash decisions.

The most common forms of cold storage are a USB 'hardware' wallet like a Ledger Nano S or a Trezor. I personally don't use them, because I know that anything electronic can still be hacked, so I prefer to go old school and use 'paper' wallets. This is where you just store your private key on a piece of paper and then safely store that bit of paper.

What are hot and cold wallets?

The way I view hot and cold wallets is to imagine I'm buying diamonds in a market square in an edgy, unfamiliar town. You feel everyone watching you as you buy your diamonds and put them in your wallet. You could walk around town with the diamonds in your wallet; it's nice and convenient to have them on you in case you want to sell them quickly, but you also run the risk of being mugged. A safer solution is to get home as soon as possible and store them in your basement safe that's bolted to the ground. That's the equivalent of a cold wallet.

The hard-drive myth

As the price of Bitcoin rises, you will see multiple articles on how someone has X amount of Bitcoin stuck in a computer or hard drive that they threw out years ago and how it's now worth X millions. The thing that's lost in translation is that the Bitcoin aren't actually in the hard drive.

When you buy a Bitcoin or any other crypto, the cryptos don't move anywhere. They remain in the Bitcoin network. Imagine that the ceiling above you right now is the Bitcoin network. All you're getting is a private key, which is simply a portal allowing you to see/have access to your Bitcoin. So in the cases of lost hard drives, all that's in there is the private key, and whoever has the private key owns them. Finders keepers, I guess.

Exchanges

The fiat exchange

This is the bane of every crypto investor. Since Day 1, the task of 'getting your money in' (converting your pounds/euros/dollars, etc. into cryptos) has been an utter chore. You typically have to open an account with a fiat exchange, go through their verification process, send your currency from your bank account to their bank account (hopefully you're not sending money to a scammer), wait anything from one to six weeks, and then finally get the funds in your account. This type of exchange is what's called a 'fiat exchange', a place where you can convert fiat to cryptos. There aren't many out there, they're difficult to set up, and the selection of cryptos you can buy through them is normally limited, meaning you end up buying Bitcoin, Ether or Litecoin and then sending them over to a 'crypto exchange'.

The crypto exchange

A crypto exchange is simply an exchange that deals only with cryptos. No fiat. When you hear statistics such as 99 per cent of crypto exchanges have been hacked, it's quite alarming. But it's worth noting that nearly all of those hacks were on crypto exchanges, not fiat exchanges. This is because fiat exchanges accept fiat currencies, they have to jump through many regulatory hoops, and they have the same level of security as a traditional share-trading platform. That's why you have to go through their laborious verification process because you're going through Know Your Customer and anti-money-laundering checks.

It doesn't look good for crypto exchanges, does it? And you'd be quite right not to trust them. I certainly don't. As I mentioned earlier, it's like buying diamonds in a dodgy town square. But the upside to crypto exchanges is that you will have a vast array of different cryptos to choose from.

With all of this in mind, you're probably a bit confused on how all of these elements fit in. So here is the simple Buy & Exit process for cryptos.

The buying and selling process

The simple way to buy cryptos is as follows:

1 Send fiat to a fiat exchange. I use Kraken, Coinbase and Bitstamp.
2 Use your fiat to buy Bitcoin.
3 Send your Bitcoin to a crypto exchange. I use Binance, Bittrex and Kucoin predominantly, but I'm adaptable here as exchanges come and go.
4 Use your Bitcoin to buy whatever altcoins you want.
5 Send all your cryptos from your exchange to a cold wallet for safe storage.

> Never, ever, trust an exchange to store your cryptos. I speak to thousands of people and you'd be surprised at how many self-taught crypto investors leave their cryptos on the exchange. It's downright foolish, and you're simply playing with fire if you do so.

1 Make detailed notes of what you bought, how much and at what price. Basic bookkeeping/logging is crucial for tax purposes.
2 Come back to sell everything just before the bubble pops!

That's it. Hopefully, it looks pretty straightforward once you see it all laid out like that. Once you've done all of this, it's worth having a weekly check-up on www.cointelegraph.com to keep abreast of what's happening in the crypto sphere.

Then, once it's time to exit, here's what you do:

1 Send your cryptos from their respective wallets over to a crypto exchange.
2 Sell everything. By default, you'll end up with Bitcoin as you buy and sell altcoins against Bitcoin.
3 Send your Bitcoin to a fiat exchange.
4 Sell your Bitcoin into whichever fiat you wish.
5 Send your fiat from your fiat exchange over to your bank account.
6 Update your trading/investing logs for tax purposes.
7 Browse the Internet for your new Lamborghini.

22

The top cryptos to get into right now

One of the questions I'm asked all the time is 'What are your top five cryptos?' A little part of me cringes each time because there's so much information I want to convey to explain why this is a silly question. But, even if I did, it would fall on deaf ears because everyone, especially in the crypto space, is out to become a zillionaire in the next two weeks!

Yes, there will be a few more wonder coins like Verge, which grew 1 million per cent in 12 months, or Stratis, which grew 65,000 per cent in six months. But, for every unicorn like that, there are more than a thousand that don't make it.

My crypto successes have also intensified the frequency of my hearing this question. I publicly called and bought into NEO at $5, ETH at $8, THC at $0.005, XVG at $0.006, XRP at $0.09, TRX at $0.02 and ADA at $0.02, and more. All of these made my community thousands of per cent ROI and, combined with my real-time alerts, my community made over £3 million profit in 2017.

Also, my favourite coins are not set in stone. I'm an investor first and foremost and, like any switched-on investor, you need to be completely cool, calm and unattached to any asset or invest-ment. The moment you allow any form of emotion to creep in, it's game over. You'll find yourself clutching a dying or dead coin, still hoping it will 'moon'. Therefore I remain objective and will drop a coin in an instant if I'm sure it's about to become a dud.

That is why I hate giving my top five coins. In one or six months or in a year it could be completely different and the peo-ple who heard my old top five could be in trouble down the line.

A potential portfolio

If you look at my past YouTube videos, you may see that in some of them I advocate buying the top 50 or 200 cryptos in order to have a good shot of bagging a winner. I likened it to having table of scratch cards in front of you, knowing that one of them was a winner. What would you do? You'd buy them all, of course.

My advice has changed a fair bit since then. Not that this was bad advice (if you did it, you'd be several thousand per cent up), but the market has evolved a lot since late 2016 and 2017 and there are better ways to go about it.

Until 2017 there really was only one type of crypto and that was a currency crypto: Bitcoin, Litecoin, Dogecoin and other first-generation cryptos. Now that we have leaped up to third generation within a year or so, the market has changed immeasurably. As I have mentioned, there are now multiple categories, so by simply buying the top 50 cryptos based on market cap, you're not getting a proper snapshot of the market, as 20 of them may be currencies.

So here is a framework portfolio, and some strategies you can start with and tweak as you identify which suit you best.

The Cryptonian Portfolio

I call my students 'Cryptonians' and this is the Cryptonian Portfolio:

- 30% HODLers
- 30% Cashflowers
- 20% Smart Tracker
- 10% Aggressive Crypto-ing
- 5% Aggressive Trading
- 5% BTC Pension.

Warning

Below I will be sharing examples of cryptos that I have bought or am buying in the following strategy/portfolio allocation explanations, but these are not set in stone and I regularly jump in and out of certain cryptos or abandon some completely. Remember, the key underpinning value driver of *every* currency, be it in pounds Sterling or cryptos, is *confidence*. Lose the confidence of the users and value and prices will soon plummet.

30% HODLers

The term 'HODL' originated from a Reddit thread, where some crypto investor was trying to write a message to everyone about how he was keeping his cool and that he was holding on to his cryptos during the bear market in 2013. The title to his message was 'I am HODLING'. Within hours an epic thread and meme was born, and now HODL is the crypto term for 'holding on for dear life'!

So if you're a HODLer, you simply don't care about the intra-day or intra-week oscillations and noise of the market because you have your portfolio, you have the bigger picture and you're HODLing until you're a millionaire.

What I've found through my own experience and via the 2,500 crypto students I have is that, when you start out, you tend to go out and buy as many cryptos as possible. You then end up with 50-plus cryptos that are a nightmare to store and secure properly as it takes a while to cold-store each one. Over time, people tend to settle for the simpler life and have a portfolio of five to ten solid cryptos with real-world utility and great prospects. That way it's easier to manage, monitor and exit in a speedy fashion when you need to.

I once sold over 200 different cryptos before a temporary crash and it took me about an hour. And in a crash, an hour can seem like an eternity! Back in August 2015 during the Black Monday crash, I was in a few trades and sitting nicely on £650 k profit when I saw the bottom and decided to close all of my trades to take profit. Due to the software taking about ten seconds to close all my trades, during which time the market was pulling back, I ended up with £426 k profit. I lost out on £224 k of pure profit due to 'slippage'. For this reason I'm now predominantly a cash-flowing HODLer. I have about 10–15 solid cryptos, most of which have a cash flow and I can exit everything in a flash if I want.

Now I know this seems to counter my own advice a little. I'm suggesting you do the Cryptonian Portfolio but I'm doing something different. It's just because I'm in a different position now. I've already made my big percentage profits and am taking a more relaxed approach. What I'm doing now won't make as much profit as the Cryptonian Portfolio.

Last point, I've put 30 per cent here for HODLers, meaning that you simply put 30 per cent of your total portfolio to HODLers. If you have a total of £1,000, then put £300 into these.

My HODLers are: NEO, ADA, TRX, VET, ONT, NEX, ETHOS, OMG, PHORE and NANO

30% Cashflowers

Cashflowers are cryptos that spit out a daily, monthly or yearly cash flow. This is important because the magic bullet to becoming financially independent is to become obsessed with, and acquire, as many cash-flowing assets as possible.

Now you're probably wondering how on earth a crypto can pay out a dividend of some sort. Most of the time it's from a 'proof of stake' type crypto where you can acquire a certain amount of a particular crypto and 'stake' it. This means that you effectively just put the crypto in a special wallet and leave it there as that wallet then helps the network to validate transactions. In return for parking your capital, you earn more of that crypto as a reward. Staking ROI ranges from 5 to 20 per cent per year on average.

There are also Masternodes. In a slightly more intensive version of staking, you have to buy many cryptos – 10,000–20,000 normally – and park them in a special wallet that is constantly connected to the network. You may have to have your computer or virtual computer always on and connected.

The ROI for Masternodes can be huge, as in from 2,080 per cent per year, or more in some cases. Unfortunately, many cryptos are created *just* to be Masternode tokens – and this is a scam/ponzi. Masternode coins have to actually be in demand and use, like DASH or PHR. You will earn a set amount of coins per day or month but if that crypto is dropping in price, it's pointless to Masternode it.

If you set up a DASH Masternode when DASH first created this concept, you needed 1,000 DASH, which was about $3,000. Now DASH is $300-ish and that same Masternode is now worth $300,000 and produces 5.8 DASH per month, which is a good $1,740 monthly income for the 4,676 DASH Masternodes out there. You can have a look at all the Masternodes and their stats at www.masternodes.pro

There are also cryptos that act like a share of a company and yield the token of their network as their dividend. This might sound confusing, so let's look at NEO.

I know you should never become affectionate towards any asset, but NEO has been very good to me and my community since I got thousands of people into it at around $6–8. When you buy NEO, you are effectively buying a share of the NEO network. For the operation of the NEO network, it uses a token called GAS as its fuel/blood. If you buy 1 NEO, you'll earn roughly 0.0003 GAS per day. It's not a lot, but if you have, say, 250 NEO, you'll be earning 0.0712 GAS per day or 2.2 per month. As an ROI right now, it's pretty poor at 3 per cent per year (at current prices). But if NEO goes to $1,500, as I'm confident it will eventually, GAS (which hovers around 50 per cent of the price of NEO) will be worth $750. If you're earning 2.2 GAS per month, that's a nice $1,650 per month residual income stream.

You can see the NEO/GAS stats/payouts here: www.neo-togas.com Other cryptos similar in nature to NEO that cash-flow like this are ONT and VET.

Another type of crypto that are Cashflowers are exchange coins like Binance and NEX. If you hold BNB or NEX, then you will get a small cut of the daily trading volume. Again, it's worth getting these exchange coins early before they increase in price and trading volume.

Now I'm cringing a little here again because, while I'm recommending that you put 10 per cent into Cashflowers, I've got a totally different percentage allocation. I'm pretty much 90 per cent into Cashflowers, but you have to understand that my portfolios are at a completely different stage from most people's holdings. I've already made over 4,000 per cent growth on my whole portfolio. The average investor makes 7 per cent per year so I've already made 571 years' worth of investing profits in the space of a year. That's mainly due to the Cheapies and the Aggressives part of my portfolio. Now I'm all about ease, simplicity, agility and residual income streams. This is why

I have 10–15 cryptos now and the bulk of my money in Cash-flowers, which spit out a beautiful income stream that I then use to acquire more cryptos. I hope this makes sense.

My Cashflowers are NEO, SMART, ONT, VET and NEX, and I have a few different Masternodes, mainly with PHR.

20% Smart Tracker

The crypto market is now broad and is continuing to broaden. This means that simply buying the top 50 or 200 coins now isn't the most efficient of methods any more. For that reason, with this Smart Tracker strategy, you simply buy two or three of the top cryptos within each crypto category. That way you are fully benefiting from the rise of the crypto market as a whole.

As I'm writing this in Q1 2018, your Smart Tracker strategy could include these:

Currency	–	NANO, XRP, LTC
General-purpose platform	–	LSK, ETH, NEM
Distributed storage	–	MAID, SC
Distributed computing	–	GNT
Privacy	–	XSPEC, PIVX, ART
Prediction	–	GNO, REP
IOT	–	MIOTA
Exchanges	–	NEX, BNB, COB
Application development	–	ARDR, STRAT, ARK
Identity	–	CVC
Payment platform	–	PAY, MTL
Lending/Crowdfunding	–	PPT, SALT

10% Aggressive Crypto-ing

I have a statistician on my team and, after much portfolio modelling and number crunching, we found that the average crypto growth from inception to 20 December 2017 was 59,601 per cent ROI. That is not a typo. That's when you exclude Bitcoin. When you include Bitcoin with this statistic, it increases it to 952,445 per cent ROI. But obviously Bitcoin is an outlier, so I'm ignoring it. What this data set shows is that with the top 50 coins in terms of market cap, from live listing to 20 December, the average growth was 59,601 per cent.

Now this is where it gets a bit murky. There's a well-known fallacy that new market dabblers fall into, and that's the belief that a stock that is £1 is much better to buy than a stock that is £10. We naturally think that the dearer stock has already done its growth or is harder to 10X from where it is compared with the cheaper stock. So people flock into the cheaper stock, hoping to snatch that elusive '10 Bagger'. This is why newbies flock to the penny stock market.

This line of thought is silly, of course, and price appreciation is completely down to the stock. Avoiding 'expensive' stocks, or even cryptos for that matter, could sting you down the line. Amazon climbed from around $8 in 1997 to $1,600 in 2018. And Warren Buffett's company Berkshire Hathaway climbed from $7,000 in 1990 to $323,000 in 2018.

However – you guessed it – there's a big *but* here. With cryptos, there is an exception to the cheap asset fallacy. As we are at the beginning of the crypto market, with thousands of new cryptos coming online every year, this is the genesis of what is most likely the biggest bull market the world has ever seen – one that will go down in history. And there are a lot of potential profits to be grabbed from getting in on some 'cheap' cryptos.

There are two main reasons for this:

1 **The potential price increase is far greater in newer cryptos (which invariably launch at a low price).**
This is because Price = Market Cap ÷ Circulating Supply. As circulating supply is inelastic and slow moving, when a particular crypto gets an influx of capital, the price quickly zooms up. This has happened time and time again when celebrities endorse a coin, making the price shoot up. If a new crypto launches at $0.10 with a market cap of $10 million, if the market cap went up to $100 million, the price will (all things being equal) rise to $1. A nice 10X gain there.

However, if you get into an older crypto – that is, say, $10 with a market cap of $10 billion – in order for that coin to 10X, its market cap will have to increase from an already high level to $100 billion. As the global crypto market cap is sitting at around $400 billion as I type this, for an individual crypto to suddenly find an extra $90 billion in market cap in a short period of time is extremely unlikely. However, a crypto going from $10 million to $100 million happens *all* the time.

2 **Investing and trading are all about gaming the psychology of the dabblers and idiots of the markets.**
I used to be a class-A idiot, so I know how they think. And because most market idiots are flocking to cheaper cryptos (for the wrong reason), you can simply game that mentality/market action and get in on these 'Cheapies' knowing that, over the next few years, the mass public is going to stampede into this industry and hoover up all the Cheapies, which will balloon the prices of your portfolio!

These are the two reasons why I like buying up some Cheapies and why you should, too. But a quick note on buying criteria: try to stick to sub-$0.20 coins, $5–50 million market cap and a *minimum* daily volume of $250 k. Here's why:

- **Price:** By getting into really cheap cryptos, you'll have loads of coins. Once it's risen and you want to take some profits off the table or even your original investment, you can do so, but you'll still be left with a lot of coins – free coins, effectively. If that coin ever really booms and explodes in price, then those 'free coins' you have will be sweet icing on your cake. For example, if you bought $1,000 worth of Ether back in early 2017 when it was $8, you'd have 125 Ether. Let's say you sold $1,000 worth when it was $50, so it's a 'risk-free' investment, you'd sell 20 Ether and be left with 105 Ether: 105 'free' Ether. Fast-forward ten months and Ether rises to $1,000, so those 105 Ether are now worth $105 k. Not bad!

- **Market cap:** You really don't want to be playing around with cryptos below $5 million in market cap. If you do, you're exposing your capital into a crypto that might not even succeed due to lack of traction. However, above the $5 million market cap, your crypto has a fighting chance. Imagine getting in on a coin like NEO when it was $5 million market cap and $0.10, which it was in January 2017. Just 11 months later it grew from $5 million to $10.5 billion and to a price of $150.

- **Minimum daily volume:** This is a very important metric to look at when evaluating a Cheapie. Your Cheapie may look like the best thing ever, but if there is little daily trading volume, you won't ever be able to sell your holdings. A minimum of $250 k daily volume really is a minimum for me. I prefer it to be in the millions as this shows that there are a lot of people using it and constantly trading it. You also have to look at how much volume there is for that particular crypto on the exchange where you wish to buy or sell it. Remember, if you want to sell an amount of cryptos, there has to be someone else or a collection of people also wanting to buy that crypto at that price. It's no different from eBay or Gumtree.

Here's a bit of a horror story I experienced to highlight the point. Back in February 2018 I tried to sell $300,000 worth of a crypto called DGD. I was selling at near all-time highs (which was great), but I got 'slipped' big time. Slippage is a term where you aim to buy or sell at one price but due to liquidity you get 'filled' at a completely different price. You get positive and negative slippage. In my case, it was dreadful slippage as I tried to sell 637 DGD at $500 ($318,500), but due to the poor liquidity on the exchange at the time and the time of night, I ended getting filled at $413.20 and getting $264,208.40. That's a $55,291.60 difference! I wasn't too annoyed as that trade still netted me $23,480 profit … but if I had been able to sell at the price I clicked, it would have been a $77,771.60 profit trade! Urgh!

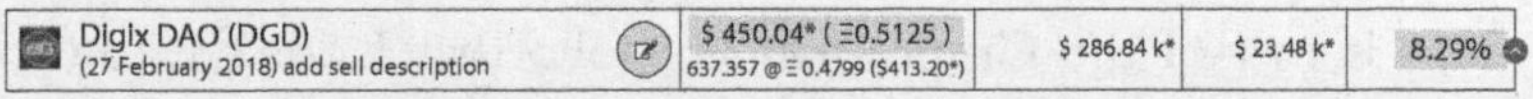

| DigIx DAO (DGD)
(27 February 2018) add sell description | | $ 450.04* (Ξ0.5125)
637.357 @ Ξ 0.4799 ($413.20*) | $ 286.84 k* | $ 23.48 k* | 8.29% |

FIGURE 22.1 Screenshot of a trade

There's an important warning here: the 'Aggressives' strategy isn't suited to most people. It's really only for those who already know how to trade the markets successfully *or* those within my crypto community who get my crypto trade alerts.

I am aggressive on cryptos that are about to break out to the upside for quick short-term profits. I identify these through technical analysis, which is the study and interpretation of charts. For instance, if I see a crypto that is looking ripe for an explosive move, I just buy the crypto and then normally sell half once it has doubled in price. This means that I get my initial investment back and I'm left with a bunch of 'free' cryptos. If it's unlikely that the crypto is going to double, then I exit at a high probability target.

This strategy is the main reason I have grown my personal and corporate portfolios by many magnitudes greater than the average HODLer out there.

My nickname for these set-ups is a Cheapie looking likely to surge. There have been many times where I've got into a nice Cheapie and it's gone up several thousand per cent. For instance, I got into TRX at $0.02, NEO at $6, ADA at $0.02, XRP at $0.02, XVG at $0.005, and many more. The bonus of being aggressive on Cheapies is that even if you fail on many of them, all it takes is for one to really rally and you've won. With TRX I managed to get about 4 million of them and when I exited my original investment, I was still left with around 2 million TRX, which is nice. I then just park it and HODL.

5% Aggressive Trading

This is part of the Cryptonian Portfolio that I don't recommend for the majority of people as it involves trading. I've been trading for 13 years now and it took me a good six years before

I was consistently profitable. So this section is really for my trading students. But what I do is trade cryptos when they are able to make low-risk, high-probability outcome moves, up or down. The benefit of this is that if a crypto goes up, if I own that crypto, not only will I profit as the value goes up, but by going 'long' and trading it, I will compound those profits. On the flipside, if I see a crypto going down, what I can then do is sell and exit that crypto, trade it by going 'short' and make profit as the crypto falls, and then, when the fall has ended, buy back the crypto and also use the profits from trading it to buy more of that crypto at the now subdued price. It's beautiful! This is how, despite the crypto market crashing over 70 per cent in the last few months (at the time of writing), I've actually managed to double my token/coin holdings. So when the global market cap goes back to previous highs, my portfolio will be worth double the previous amount.

For those still unsure, yes, you can trade and profit from falling and rising markets even if you don't own the cryptos. It's a bit like 'betting' on a horse to win or lose a race. You don't own the horse or the jockey, but you're simply profiting on the movement of the horse.

If active trading isn't suitable for you, that's great. Just redirect this 5 per cent to another section of the Cryptonian Portfolio such as the Smart Tracker section for instance. But for those who are keen and interested in up-levelling your knowledge, it's worth checking out www.TheRealisticTrader.com/ultimate-trading-video-course Here I've basically put everything I know about trading in a comprehensive video course including all of my strategies. This is so that, when I eventually die, my children will be able to learn what I knew.

5% Bitcoin Pension

People often bill me online as a 'Bitcoin hater'. This is far from the case. I have tremendous respect for Bitcoin as it has sparked this amazing new market and paradigm shift from centralized powers to decentralized entities which will eventually lead to much more efficient markets, smaller governments and cheaper prices for the things we buy and consume. But after crunching thousands of statistical models, it's now evident that if your sole goal is portfolio maximization, then you should not hold Bitcoin. In terms of future potential percentage growth, it's now the crypto with the gammy leg holding up the rest of the pack as it's already grown over 3.3 million per cent. So it's already done its main growth spurt in percentage terms. However, if your goal is crypto wealth preservation, then definitely hold Bitcoin. It's never been hacked, has been around since 2009 and is the most battle-tested of all other cryptos.

So really it all depends on your goals. The Cryptonian Portfolio is designed using maths and is the best combination of security along with maximizing your potential growth. Also by having just a small portion of Bitcoin, it also acts as a bit of a 'punt' just in case Bitcoin does grow to the lofty heights of $1 million per Bitcoin as many crypto experts and big names believe. This is why I've given a Bitcoin to each of my sons as their own DIY pension just in case Bitcoin does grow to those levels. After all, there will only ever be 21 million Bitcoin in existence, and it's estimated that it will cost billions to mine that 21 millionth Bitcoin. Also, the price of Bitcoin historically sits around 2.5 times the cost of mining. As the price of Bitcoin mining can be calculated, and if this 2.5-times constant remains, it's likely that, by the end of 2019, the price of Bitcoin could be worth over $50 k. And in excess of $500 k by 2025 ...

23
Ten mistakes most crypto novices make

This and the next chapter present a quick broad-brush overview of common mistakes that newcomers to crypto make. Even if you're already an experienced trader or HODLer, I'm sure there are at least one or two nuggets you can take away from these that will help your future profits.

Mistake 1: Day trading

Day trading is the devil (for beginners).

At least 90 per cent of all traders lose money. It's a frightening fact. The number of traders emerging these days is increasing dramatically with the advent of cheap, fast Internet connections, cheaper computers and free trading software. But the reason why such a high percentage of people consistently lose money is day trading.

Day trading is where you place dozens of trades per day and close all of your trades by the end of the day. In order to day-trade, you typically need to spend hours with your eyes glued to your screen and, by the end of the day, your eyes will be exhausted, your brain will be fried, and normally your trading account will have taken a battering. And people actually try to day-trade with cryptos. It's crazy, especially as there's so much manipulation going on in this market and it's already like penny stocks on steroids and heroin at the same time!

Trading is, and should be, a life skill, which makes day trading completely unsustainable, as you'll either fizzle out mentally or run out of money, or both. For some reason, whenever money is involved, your heightened emotions are amplified and this is made worse if you're in a losing position. You fool yourself that it'll come back round, so you opt to let it run overnight.

Not a good idea. You'll be checking your trades every half an hour and you'll be drained in every possible way, which will make your next day of trading hopeless.

Even if you can manage all that or you're not doing too badly (everyone gets a winning streak), day trading is extremely hard to fit into the rest of your life. Most people have either a full-time job or run their own business, so you'll be working a minimum of eight hours a day. Where are you going to find three to five more hours a day for day trading? If you do give it a go, I'm sure you'll eventually agree with me that day trading is extremely hazardous to your trading account and to your health.

If it's so bad, why does everyone do it?

It's a good question. It's mainly down to the Internet and a distinct lack of information, education and training. What normally happens is that people google how to trade and almost every single search result they find is from a trading broker or trading training provider promoting day trading. As a result, it's all people ever know. And the reason day trading is so heavily promoted is because of the commissions or spreads it generates.

For example, let's take the UK stock market, the FTSE 100. If, let's say, the price is 6,790 and you want to buy it and 'go long' (which means you hope it goes up), the price your broker will likely give to you will be 6,792. The spread (the difference between those two prices) in this example is two points. The average position size is £10 per point. So your broker has immediately made two points (£20) in profit, regardless of whether you win or lose your trade. They want people to make as many trades as possible so that they get more commissions and spreads. There are lots of commissions to be made, which is why so many Internet marketers promote opening a live trading account through their affiliate link. That way, every time someone places a trade, they get a kickback.

Siam's tips

- **Avoid day trading like the plague.** This includes the new form of trading scam out there called Binary Options. Nearly all the trading training companies on Google teach you how to day-trade, but avoid them at all costs. They are just common day scams.
- **Don't ever think that you are different and that you can make it work.** Even if you're a seasoned poker player, I promise you that you won't. Day trading should be explored only once you've got at least three or four years of successful trading under your belt. Otherwise it's like getting a 17-year-old learner driver to race in the Grand Prix in an F1 car … it's going to end in tears.
- **Find someone who is trusted and respected and get tuition from them.** Make sure, of course, that they are not teaching day trading! Most of what you see on the Internet about trading is just marketing or cons.
- **Remember that anything below the four-hour chart is just noise.** Day trading involves looking at 1-, 5-, 15- and 60-minute charts for hours on end. You need to stick to the daily charts!
- **Remember, it makes no sense to chain yourself to trading screens every day.** People trade because they want one day to have more time and freedom, not less, so doing this is completely incompatible with your goals.

Mistake 2: Acting on your emotions

> Having emotions while trading/investing is one of the quickest ways to blow your account.

Women make the best traders/investors. They soar above men because they can work dispassionately. They can completely desensitize when it comes to trading. They tend not to have the big ego that's characteristic of many men and they don't let their emotions cloud their judgement. As a result, female traders are calm, calculated and methodical. They're less likely to shoot from the hip just because their gut is telling them to sell.

When you trade you must not have *any* emotions. Not one. Your frame of mind needs to be free of greed, anger, frustration, ego, revenge, and also excitement and hope. If you have any emotions, you'll trade in damaging ways, with revenge the deadliest of them all. If you've lost a big wad of money on a trade and you succumb to revenge, you'll begin to trade recklessly by trying to immediately 'win' back all your money. You'll do crazy things like placing too many trades or even 'doubling-down'. Even a seasoned gambler would say that this is the worst thing you can do, as it's just a downward spiral of despair.

Siam's tips

- **Don't act on the markets if you're feeling emotional.** There shouldn't be any fear, hope, greed or anger. If your state of mind is anything other than calm neutrality, don't trade. This may all sound silly but your mood really does reflect the types of trades you place, and you're more likely to stray from your trading plan (more on this later).

- **If you do find yourself trading emotionally, mitigate your risk.** Immediately close your positions or, at the very least, tighten up your stop losses .Then turn off your computer and go for a walk. Just do anything but trade/invest.
- **Remember that you need to be a cold, calm, logically thinking robot.** *Star Trek*'s Lieutenant Commander Data is the perfect trading role model.

What's a stop loss?

For the uninitiated, a stop loss is simply a feature where you can determine the maximum amount of risk you're willing to accept. So if you place a trade and you're only willing to lose a maximum of £50 on that trade, you can set up a stop at that level. So, if the trade goes against you, the moment you're £50 down, the trade will automatically close. So it's great for risk mitigation. but on the flipside you can use your stop to lock in profits. So let's say you're £500 in profit on a trade, and you want to lock in, say, £300 if anything were to go wrong. You can simply move your stop to the level where, if your profitable trade were to drop to £300 of profit, the trade would automatically close.

Mistake 3: Over-trading and boredom trading

Boring trading is good trading.

Over-trading is a standard beginner's mistake. Excitement and greed go hand in hand with trading and often result in people either placing far too many trades all at once or trading all the time. Whether it's morning, noon or night, rookies will be bea-vering away placing dozens of trades. Not only is this a great way to lose money from spreads, taxes or commission charges every time you place a trade, but it's also hard to productively monitor all of those trades. Over-trading exposes you to a lot of risk. If you're too trigger-happy, reacting to every news item that could affect a stock, you'll make mistakes. Before you know it, your trading account is hammered or wiped out.

You don't always have to be in a trade. This took me a long time to understand. Your trading capital is sacred and the number-one rule of trading is capital preservation. Profits are just a bonus that comes with the activity. Be stringent about when and what you invest or trade in. Throwing as much mud as possible at a wall and hoping some of it sticks is not a good method of preserving your capital.

Boredom trading is another money drain. If you're bored and you go searching for something to buy or sell, you'll most likely lower your standards when picking your trade. If you're bored, don't trade. And don't place trades 'just for fun'. It's for your own safety ...

Siam's tips

- **Be a sniper, not a machine gunner.** Snipers lie in wait until their target is in sight and then act. And snipers have a much higher hit rate than machine gunners. Trading is all about low risk/high probability outcome trades. You need to target the peachy low-hanging fruit, so when you see it, you take it. You really must *never* be a machine gunner when you're trading. Placing loads of trades and hoping something hits is not a good tactic, so don't 'spray and pray'.

- **If you're bored, don't go looking for random cryptos to buy.** This is most likely to mean that you lose by lowering your standards when picking your trade.
- **Try to limit the amount of trades you have on at any one time.** But if you're investing, the number of cryptos you hold doesn't matter too much.

> The number-one objective with trading and gambling is **capital preservation**.

Mistake 4: Poor risk management

> Risk management is the *single most important* aspect of trading. Without it you are certain to fail every time you enter the market.

Combined with over-trading and not using stop losses, poor risk management is one of the main reasons so many people get chewed up by the markets, only to quit and forever call trading 'gambling'. One of the classic examples of poor risk management is 'betting' too much per trade. To continue with the gambling theme, if you went to a casino with £100 to play with and put it all on 'black', this would be poor risk management. If you lose, you're out, and if you're out of the game, you can't make any profits.

Now let's say that you wised up to this and returned the next day with another £100 but this time you put only £25 on black. This is a better strategy than before, as it would take a few bad losses before you'd be out, but it's still dreadful risk management.

In some of my seminars I tell the audience to imagine having £5,000 in a trading account and then I ask them how much they would risk on a trade they were confident about. The answers vary from £500 all the way up to £5,000, but no one ever gets it right.

While the majority of answers fall in the £1,000–£3,000 range, even the conservative people who say £500 are still far off the mark when it comes to risk management. At that level, you just need ten bad losses and your account would be wiped out. The answer I'm looking for is … £12.50! Yes, £12.50 is all you should risk on that trade. The unwritten rule all beginners *need* to stick to is the 0.25 per cent rule:

Never risk more than 0.25 per cent of your total capital per trade.

In fact, if you ask some experienced veteran traders, even they would say they barely risk more than 0.5 per cent, regardless of how confident they are before entering a trade. I cannot stress how important this rule is. It's the single most important thing to remember when you are trying to preserve your capital.

I tend to trade 0.1–0.25 per cent maximum risk and I still consistently make well over 10–20 per cent per year. This is because, if you were to lose ten trades in a row, risking even just 1 per cent you would be 9.48 per cent down. That's just pushed you back a year!

Many people will be thinking, 'That's way too small, I'll hardly make any money trading that small a position. I'll trade a little bit bigger to play it safe.' OK, how much bigger? Let's say 5 per cent. At that level, with ten straight losing trades, instead of being 9.48 per cent down, you'd be 40.13 per cent down. That's a devastating blow to your account. That would set you back three to five years.

When you trade at 0.25 per cent maximum risk, in order to have a 10 per cent drawdown, you would need to lose 40 trades in a row. That's extremely unlikely.

Another thing to think about with risk management is your RRR – your risk-to-reward ratio. In short, you need to make sure that your rewards are at the very least *twice* that of your losses. I'll spare you the maths, but what that means is that out of every ten trades, you could totally lose six of them and still be in profit.

Just to repeat that, you can have just a 40 per cent success rate and still be in profit. Not bad, eh?

Siam's tips

- **Always stick to the 0.25 per cent rule.** This should be your maximum; go lower if you can. I make 90 per cent of my trades at 0.25 per cent maximum risk.
- **Try your absolute hardest to maintain a 1:2 RRR.** Your wins need to always double your losses. In the long run, a 1:2 RRR will really look after you. One of the reasons casinos are extremely lucrative is that the odds are always in favour of 'the House'. In some cases, their odds are only a couple per cent in their favour, but it doesn't matter. It's a numbers game and, in the long run, the House always wins.
- **Protect and preserve your capital as if it's your only kidney.**
- **You can ignore these tips if you're investing in cryptos for the long term.** For example, there's absolutely nothing wrong with splitting your money up into 10 per cent chunks and investing in ten super-solid cryptos with real-world utility and riding it all out for years.

Mistake 5: Trading with the wrong mindset

You are *not* going to make a killing today ...

What tends to happen when people start out is that, very early on, they have a winning streak. Whether it's beginner's luck or natural innate ability, it's the worst thing that could possibly happen to you. You will think you're Gordon Gecko of Wall Street, about to set the world on fire with your trading prowess. Except that it's almost always followed by a catastrophic loss in which you'll end up giving back all your new profits, along with the rest of the money you started out with.

I've done this four times. I used to think I was smart, but now I just cringe when I look back. If this has already happened to you, don't worry. The best thing to do right now is to learn from your mistakes and find out why your trades went against you. You'll probably find that it was a combination of some of the mistakes covered in this book. Don't ignore what happened and blame the markets. The markets aren't wrong ... you are. And the only things you're lacking are the correct information, education and training.

I've done a lot of reading and listened to some of the best traders in the world, past and present, and one of the remarkable things I've learned is that most of them actually feared the markets. With that fear, though, came a sense of respect. They knew that, like a minefield, one wrong move would ruin their trade or trading account. The trick was to absorb as much knowledge and experience as they could. If you follow in their footsteps, you'll eventually learn what a 'buried mine' looks like.

The knowledge bit is the easy part, as you can read as much as you like. But the experience part can be developed only through actual hands-on trading. Like flying a helicopter, you could know the instruction manuals off by heart, but until you've put in the flying time, you won't be able to hold a stable hover. Once you learn it, you'll never forget.

So fear and respect the markets, and be in the correct mindset before trading. As mentioned above (see Mistake 2), your mind should be calm and neutral and feeling absolutely no emotion. I have a trick that's been with me for years. I have a note on my whiteboard in front of my trading station. It reads, 'Siam, today you're going to lose ... and you're going to lose BIG.' This is probably contrary to what every sports coach/psychologist would recommend, as sportsmen and women need to go into 'battle' with a positive mindset, but with trading it's the right approach. I guarantee that if you start your day of trading with a happy 'I'm going to make a killing today' attitude, you'll lose ... and you'll lose big.

Even worse is starting the day with a monetary target you want to hit. All this will do is unconsciously make you place substandard trades or over-trade to achieve your targets. That note simply humbles me and prevents those horns of greed from emerging.

Siam's tips

- **Realize that any winning streak early on isn't going to last for long and that you must preserve your capital at all costs.** If you do get a winning streak early on in your trading, congratulations! Trading is exhilarating when you're winning, but please have the presence of mind to move your stop losses up to lock in some of your profits or at least break even. Also, re-analyse your trades to see what you did right.

- **If you got overconfident and lost everything,
  don't worry.** Just analyse what went wrong and treat
  the money you lost as 'learning capital'. For me, my
  'learning capital' was just over £50 k. I was stupid and
  a slow learner. Don't follow in my footsteps.
- **Set up three different types of emotion-altering
  anchors: visual, audio and kinaesthetic (seeing,
  hearing and feeling).** If you set up your 'VAK
  anchors' you can put yourself in the perfect trading
  mindset. So find your anchors; you may already have
  them without realizing. I never used to believe in this
  sort of 'stuff' but it really does work. It's why you'll
  see a lot of traders in the city wearing headphones.
  They're just listening to their audio anchors ...

Siam's anchors

For my visual anchor, I have a big whiteboard full of
my goals, dreams and aspirations, a picture of my next car
and a picture of Earth from space (one of my dreams is
to spend a few days orbiting Earth in zero gravity). These
visual stimuli remind me why I do what I do.

For my audio anchor, there's a piano piece called 'I
Giorni' by Ludovico Einaudi, which completely levels me
out. I don't listen to much classical music, but I could be
in absolutely any mood and this piece instantly returns me
to a state of equilibrium.

For my kinaesthetic anchor, I have a squishy ball on my
desk. Throwing it against the wall a few times while listening to the audio anchor always does the trick.

- **Your job is to wait and pounce when the market starts trending.** Never enter the markets with a monetary goal to accomplish for the day, week or month. It'll adversely affect your trading. Also, some weeks there may not be a single optimal trade to place. Don't worry ... the market just goes sideways sometimes.

Mistake 6: Buying Internet tips

On the markets, people's wealth is being continuously transferred from the uninformed over to the informed. It's simply a case of knowledge that will stitch up those holes in your pockets ...

You can be pretty sure that anyone who says that they 'dabble' in stocks or cryptos or any market doesn't really know what they are doing and they are most likely losing money hand over fist. And 'dabblers' *love* to buy Internet tips. Just do a search for trading or investing tips and Google will present you with hundreds of companies trying to sell you magazine subscriptions, expensive snazzy software and email alerts all promising that their tips will earn you a fortune.

Unfortunately, you will be throwing your money away if you subscribe to any of these, and you will lose even more if you act on the tips they give you. I'm sure that there are a few good ones out there, but what tends to happen is that the potential price movement has or is normally factored into the existing price. For instance, let's assume a company releases a really good report and that sales are up. Within a millisecond of that report being released, high-frequency trading robots around the world would have assimilated that data as good news and would have bought millions of dollars' worth of that stock. So, by the time you and the rest of the public are picking up on this bullish news via the Internet or even worse, the newspapers, the stock has already risen substantially. Therefore, if you act off that information, you will be buying at new highs, which isn't ideal. This is true especially where newspapers have an editorial about a stock that is 'going places'. So when the masses pile into the new 'hot stock or crypto', either nothing happens or it rises for a tiny bit before plummeting and taking all your money with it. This is what's called a 'pump and dump' scheme. It's rife in crypto forums and bulletin boards, especially the well-known and respected ones.

What happens is that a group of people pick a crypto to target. They then heavily invest in that crypto, which may start a bit of a rise and at the same time they launch a full-scale Internet campaign to ramp up the 'amazing potential of this stock'. Thousands of naive investors who don't know any better then just blindly invest. The crypto then rises quite a bit (even better for the con artists if that crypto is highlighted by a newspaper or popular website) and when it reaches the desired price target, they'll all at once sell their shares and close all positions. Before you know it, they've made a fortune and thousands of people are in extremely negative positions. It's an everyday occurrence, unfortunately. You don't get any of this with currencies, which is one reason why I predominantly trade the currency market, as no individual, group of people or company can influence the FX market due to its sheer size.

Siam's tips

- **Steer clear of anything online that promises huge returns from tips or special strategies.** Do not under any circumstances buy from these Internet marketers, who are just getting kickbacks from brokers and are not proper traders. This may seem as if I'm shooting myself in the foot, as one of the perks of belonging to my crypto community is that you get access to my private Telegram Channel, where I share every move I make. But I have to emphasize that you will *not* make consistent daily returns from this. No one can promise that, as the markets are *not* consistent. They ebb and flow. Sometimes I go weeks without doing anything.

- **Continue always to learn and enhance your skills, knowledge and experience.** Your BS detector will soon become finely tuned ...

Mistake 7: Believing in the Holy Grail trading system

> Get Rich Quick schemes *do not* work. In reality, they are Get Poorer Quicker schemes.

There are literally tens of thousands of different trading systems out there on the Internet and each system or strategy has dozens of different variants. What people tend to think is that out of that huge haystack of methods, there'll be a shiny needle that will lift their trading to glorious new heights. People spend months and years hopping from one method to the next without any real success. Sometimes they get lucky and find a method that works for them for a month, only to find that the following month it blows their account. I've done this and I've spent good money on silly systems that seemed too good to be true. Guess what? They were. The upsetting and blunt reality is that there is no Holy Grail trading system – fact.

The two industries with the largest amount of money and investment in the world are the oil sector and the finance sector. Oil is the obvious one as it's the blood of the world, which is rapidly diminishing and so sexier technology is being created to locate and extract it, but the finance sector is just as big and lucrative. Banks and other private companies spend billions on research and equipment to find out how to leech as many pennies from the financial system as possible.

What these 'big boys' have found is that by using extremely fast Internet connections and powerful computers, they can act in mere microseconds, which means they can get in front of any move about to happen. They place millions of trades per day and so this practice is called high-frequency trading (HFT). It's highly profitable for those who do it and one firm called Virtu Financial is the king of HFT. In 1,238 days of trading, they have had just one losing day. One! This company makes on average around £1 million per day.

With cryptos there aren't any HFT bots on this scale just yet, but give it time. I wouldn't be surprised if a big mover will have entered the scene by the end of 2019. As a private trader at home on your laptop, you are competing against these behemoths and some of the brightest minds in the world. You really don't stand much of a chance … unless you know what you're doing.

The financial system has morphed into a completely different beast over the last four years. The markets are now changing roughly every five years or so, which means that a successful trading system from the 2000s is likely to be redundant today. It's futile to buy a method when you have no idea how it works or the best time to use it. Some strategies may work well for commodities, but not for bonds or stocks.

Siam's tips

- **Keep on learning and seek tuition from successful traders.** I really can't stress how important financial education is. If you are embarking on a trading journey, you need to know how and why everything works. Having more knowledge really is like getting a clearer lens in your glasses. You'll bypass years of frustration and lost money this way.
- **Don't buy fancy, expensive software or special trading strategies.** You don't need special software as the free software you get with most brokers is sufficient. If a simple guy from Norwich can trade successfully and consistently with the free software on a laptop, so can you!
- **Find a strategy with a relatively consistent track record and stick to it.** Again, the more knowledge you have, the more accurate and decisive you can be when using it, because knowing when and when not to place a trade or use a tool is crucial. If you want to learn the four methods I personally use, just visit www.TheRealisticTrader.com and it will guide you on how to access them.
- **Stay away from day trading and binary options.** Most scams, cons or pleas to 'buy this super-secret strategy' are geared around these. Anyone who tries to promote the idea that you can earn between £100 and £5,000 per day is being grossly misleading and will want to teach you how to day-trade. Remember, if you're being taught to look at the 1-, 5-, 15- or 60-minute charts … run away and don't look back. This single tip will save you thousands. I trade less than five minutes a day, which is why I know I'll still

be trading for decades to come. Just try to find a bank trader older than 30 years old … you won't. Most fizzle out by the age of 29!

Mistake 8: Leaving all your cryptos in an exchange

> The dumbest thing you can do in this market …

This is what typically happens. Someone decides to get into cryptos from either peer pressure, FOMO or because they want to be an innovator. They do a bit of googling to understand the basics and, after five to ten hours of solid knowledge acquisition, feel confident enough to jump into some live action.

After setting up the accounts and faffing for a few days getting money into their new exchange, excitement is coursing through their veins and they buy, buy, buy. They feel happy. They've finally got their cryptos and the articles they've read indicate that the ones they've just bought will 'moon' very soon. They may well, but they've just committed the biggest cryptos investing error… they've left their cryptos in the exchange.

Nearly every crypto exchange ever created has been hacked or shut down, so leaving your hard-earned cryptos on any exchange is asking for trouble. Put it this way: if you're a super-hacker, would you spend 100 hours targeting an average Joe with maybe a few grand? Or would you target an exchange with tens of millions of dollars' worth of cryptos? Yes, you'd go for the bigger prize.

Siam's tip

- **Always store all your cryptos in cold storage or, at the very least, a hot wallet.** Never leave your cryptos in an exchange.

Mistake 9: Using a trading bot

> Like a moth to a flame, people still keep buying them. It's just a product for marketers to sell. Trading bots are not a solution for trading laziness.

Trading bots simply don't work. I fully understand why people buy them. They have busy, hectic lives and a demanding full-time job, so they don't have time to trade or dedicate time to learning. When a sparkly new gizmo appears on an Internet ad promising great returns after you've left the house for work, it can be appealing. Who wouldn't want some software that effectively turns your laptop into a trading cash machine while you eat, sleep and work? It's the same horns of greed that come out when people get suckered into buying the next Holy Grail trading system. Once you've started mentally spending the money you're going to make from this trading bot, it's too late. You've already been sucked into the marketing.

Here's how it works. You either download a zip file or, if the marketer is really stylish, you'll get something attractive in the post like a DVD. You have probably already been upsold during the checkout process to buy the 'secret trading strategy' that works best for this software. You install it and press go. You'll leave it running overnight, wake up the next morning only to find out it hasn't really done much, or you may even be in a slight loss. A key reason for this (other than this being a total gimmick) is that, overnight, not much really happens during the Asian session for currency trading and absolutely nothing happens for stocks. So you then give it the benefit of the doubt and leave it running all day while you go to work, only to return home later to find one of these two things has happened:

- You've lost an obscene amount of money.
- Not much has happened and you've only lost a little bit of money.

The end result is the same. You either experience the guillotine slicing of your account, or you just keep it running and slowly bleed your account with a thousand cuts. In short, don't waste your time with it.

The interesting part is that the trading strategy the bot is using may actually be a pretty handy strategy if you used it manually. In fact, you'd probably get better results. The bot will always fail miserably because it doesn't think; it just follows its set of instructions and only moves the stop loss up to the parameters it's set to. Whereas when you trade yourself, you will always be analysing the market and moving your stops to the optimum parts. Also, if you're a good trader, you will cut your losses short and let your winners run. Trading bots can't do this as well as you can.

Siam's tips

- **Don't waste your time or money on a trading bot.** Remember that they are just a marketing gimmick.
- **If you do buy one, for an experience or as an experiment, just set it up and only trade the smallest positions possible.** Then, when the bot loses a trade, you lose only small change.

- **Continue focusing on the things that really matter.** These things are your knowledge, education and training. They are what will turn into your future payday and a life of disposable income.

Mistake 10: Going into live trading rooms

If you're trading the correct way, there is no need for live trading rooms. Day trading is like Las Vegas. You get dazzled by the lights and potential riches, but most people leave Vegas poorer. Only the pros win.

The Internet is littered with live trading rooms, which are simply the webcams or screen-shares of a trader. In them, you can 'look over their shoulder' to see how they trade. Trading rooms normally come with a monthly subscription of anything upwards of £50, and you'll be surprised at how bad some of them are. I remember signing up to one trading 'guru' for two months and during those two months I just sat with the other subscribers and watched him in despair as he almost blew his whole account. Pretty much every trade he placed went against him but he always somehow managed to justify them.

If you're ever bored, it's fun to try to find the cheapest live trading room you can. If you're lucky, you'll find someone like I did who is plain awful. Then try putting some really small trades, exactly the opposite to what he's placing, and see what happens. I say 'he' because I've never come across a female trader with a live trading room. I don't know why that is, though ...

Another reason why these are a waste of your time is because you'll be watching a day trader, and I hope I've hammered into you by now that day trading is something to avoid at all costs.

Siam's tips

- **Don't waste your time copying or following a day trader, regardless of how good he/she is.** If they are genuinely good, it's because they've spent years learning their craft. You simply cannot effectively learn this in a year or less. Just like car racing, first you need to learn how to drive, then you need to learn how to manage spins and so on and then slowly work your way up to the F1 racing car. Skipping a few steps will likely result in a calamitous crash.
- **Boring trading is good trading.**

24
Eleven more mistakes made by crypto novices

As with the previous chapter, here are some more common mistakes that newcomers to crypto make. Even experienced traders will benefit from these reminders.

Mistake 11: Following email updates

> Some of the best traders in the world read and subscribe to trading email updates, only to take the opposite view.

Just like shiny new trading systems, trading bots and live trading rooms, email updates from market 'gurus' are just as common. From experience I've found that a lot of these updates come from marketers who know a little about trading (just enough to sound credible) but, when you ask a question, there is no depth of knowledge. Just analyse the emails they send and there will be a link somewhere trying to get you to open a live trading account through some broker.

There are some good ones out there, but you have to be careful and, whatever you do, don't blindly copy their trades. I've wasted thousands in the past watching a video update and becoming convinced that some currency is about to rise or fall, then placing the trade without any of my own analysis. This has never ended well. Even if you are convinced by an email or video update, just DYOR (do your own research).

Siam's tips

- **Take updates with a pinch of salt.** If you've done my course, you'll know exactly what to look for and whether or not the email/video is from a fraudster.
- **Never place a trade blindly without doing your own research.**

- **Analyse any offers carefully.** I've done a couple of marketing courses myself while learning how to grow my businesses and there's an email tactic that is widely used. It's called the 1:5 ratio. What they do is send you five really good-value emails, and then the sixth email will be a sales email. This is so that you have begun to trust them before they hit you with a sale. In the marketing/business sense this is a very good way to email your list, but when you finally receive the sales email, do properly analyse it. Is it a genuinely good offer or are they just trying to get you to open up a live account on their affiliate link?

Mistake 12: Believing the mainstream media

> *The Financial Times*, the *Telegraph* and the BBC are like the *Sunday Sport* to me. They only tell you what you want to hear – not the inconvenient truths you absolutely need to hear.

Pretty much every stat the UK Government issues is grossly misleading and often close to plain lies. The main topics they mislead the public on are inflation, GDP, unemployment and housing data. So here are the bones of it all.

Inflation

As I write this, according to the UK Government, UK inflation right now is 0.5 per cent. Now this is the most farcical of all statistics as it's becoming almost common knowledge that *real* inflation is nearer 10 per cent. The way they calculate inflation is by taking a typical 'basket of goods', things the public buy from day to day, like bread, milk, cars, iPhones and CDs. (Funnily enough, rent or housing costs are not included. They used to be, but they removed this calculation in 1983 as they started to purposely inflate the housing market.)

They then compare the prices in this basket to those of last month, last year, the last five years and so on and they plot a graph. What they fail to realize, or choose to ignore, is that *everything* in that basket is now smaller or of less value than it used to be. For example, let's take a Snickers chocolate bar (my favourite). In 2003 they cost, on average, 30p. But now they average around 60p. I've spent around 90p on one in some places. In ten years the price has increased by more than 100 per cent – *and* they are all now 7.2 per cent smaller. This same statistic applies to everything else in the basket. When you crunch the numbers, *real* inflation and *real* living costs are near double digits and are far outpacing economic growth.

Gross domestic product (GDP)

Recently, the US GDP calculations were changed: they are now including research and development (R&D) spending as part of the GDP. Now this is absurd. The USA spends more money on military R&D than every other country in the world combined. Even their medicine R&D dwarfs that of other nations. It could be argued that medicine R&D could produce more efficient medicines, which would positively bring more revenue in, but it's negligible. Military R&D has next to no productive use (other than for war), so this is a ploy to make the US debt-to-GDP ratio look better than it really is. The USA is the only country in the world to do this but it probably won't be long before the UK follows suit in order to hide our problems. In addition, GDP is an extremely flawed concept designed for the

Second World War era and I could talk for a week on why this statistic is harming the world.

Jobs/unemployment data

This is a huge topic but, in a nutshell, when calculating these figures, the UK Government is now purposely stretching the parameters of what a full-time employed person actually is. They now count people with a 'part-time job who are seeking a full-time job' as 'fully employed'. They are including some forms of part-time charity or volunteer workers and many other profiles as 'fully employed'. They're doing it at the other end of the scale as well, by classing some people without a job who are seeking employment as 'part-time' employed and so on. They're trying to make these figures show that unemployment isn't as bad as it really is, when the poor/rich divide is increasing dramatically.

Housing data

Housing data is probably as laughable as inflation data. For some reason the UK Government likes to promote to the public that a rising housing market means that the UK economy is improving. And as the public are grossly ignorant of investing matters, we just nod and accept what we see in the news. There are two points to make here:

- **The housing market is not a reflection of how our economy is doing.** There is zero correlation between rising house prices equalling a better economy. In fact, rising house prices reduce GDP. The main reason for this is that as house prices, mortgages and rent increase, they take up a larger percentage of people's monthly income. As a result, if people are spending more on rent and mortgages, they will subsequently spend less in shops, which therefore adversely affects our economy.

- **The UK Government is now openly trying to pump up this market again with 95 per cent mortgages.** When you look at US housing data, there's even more of an exaggeration. What they fail to show is that the Federal Reserve is buying up $85 billion a month of mortgage-backed securities, other toxic bonds and also at least 70,000 empty homes per month using proxies.

I hope you can now see that at the very least we need to question what we are told. Housing, employment, GDP and inflation data are rigged, and that's only the tip of the iceberg. If they are rigging interest rates (LIBOR), imagine what else they are doing.

Siam's tips

- **Check real adjusted data, not published nominal data.** Do this whenever you go to buy a mortgage, or invest in the stock market or pensions. www. ShadowStats.com is a great site for real data.
- **Try not to trade based on what you see in the news.** Most of the time, the news has already been factored into the price of your market, which is why sometimes bad news comes out but the market does nothing, or even rises.
- **If you're buying a house, be careful.** Interest rates are at 300-year lows and they can and will only rise. This will have crippling effects on the economy and the housing market. What I'm strongly suggesting to my close friends and family is that they fix their mortgage immediately, for as long as possible.

- **Make sure you explore all the videos at** www. InvestingStarterPack.com. Once you've done that, this section on macroeconomics will make far more sense.

Mistake 13: Not having risk capital

> You will absolutely need some learning capital while you develop your trading skills and experience. Just don't expect to get your learning capital back!

Everything has a price. And don't be fooled into thinking that the price is always in money. If you want to become a master knitter, the price will most likely be time in learning the skill and maybe a few bleeding thumbs. If you want to be a successful business owner or millionaire, the price you'll most definitely pay will be in time, lack of sleep, stress and a diminished friend base, as well as possibly financial.

The reason why a lot of people aren't millionaires or even wealthy is that they are not prepared to pay the price of becoming one. It's far easier to clock in at work for eight hours a day, come home to dinner then go to the pub. Most people would shudder at the thought of quietly building a part-time business from 6 p.m. to 10 p.m. alongside their full-time job and managing their family. As any entrepreneur will tell you, stopping work for the day at 7 p.m. would be an early finish.

So how serious are you at becoming consistently profitable at trading? The ultimate reward is to be able to turn your laptop into a cash machine and live the luxurious life you want with just five minutes' trading a day. The question is: are you prepared to take the time and effort to build your knowledge, to shoulder the cost of doing courses to learn from successful traders, and to spend the 12 months it takes on average to become proficient? More importantly, are you comfortable with losing a small bit of your capital? Every trader who has ever lived has lost trades, lost money and had losing streaks.

Siam's tips

- **Treat that first £2,000 as learning capital and expect to make mistakes and lose it all.** It's best to get all your learning and losing done early on. I always recommend that you stay on your simulation account until you are confident and profitable on it before opening a live £2,000 trading account. Whatever you do, analyse every error and learn from your mistakes. Even better, learn from my hiccups, described in this book.
- **Whenever you put money into your live account, it should be risk capital that you can afford to lose.** Don't put your last pound of next month's rent into your account. This is one of the silliest mistakes I've ever made and it will only result in heightened anxiety that will damage your trading performance.

Mistake 14: Not having minimum investing criteria

At least 90 per cent of all cryptos are pure BS ...

When you're investing in this beautiful but chaotic market, you need to understand that it's a market that is 1 per cent utility value and 99 per cent nonsense, scams, greed, future hopes and dreams. That's why you need to have a filter to help you gauge which cryptos to get into and not be fooled into buying some obscure crypto just because it has some cool marketing.

Also, the marketing vs developer ratio is critical. I'd much rather invest in a venture with one marketing person and 20 developers than a venture with 20 marketers and one developer.

Siam's tips

- **You need to play with cryptos that have at least a $5 million market cap.** This way your crypto has a chance of gaining traction and appreciating and carrying out its mission. This is the absolute minimum. The reason for this is that you don't want to risk your money in a venture that may never take off.
- **Make sure that there is at least $250,000 in average daily trading volume in the exchange you're aiming to buy/sell from.** There's no point in getting into some obscure crypto only not to be able to sell it in the future because no one is trading it.
- **Your crypto must be fulfilling a real-world utility or plugging an existing need/problem.** Any crypto that doesn't match this criterion is just a shitcoin.
- **The team is critical.** It's often said that a great business owner could make even a bad company profitable. And a bad business owner could ruin a great company. It's exactly the same in the crypto space. When getting into a new crypto, I always look to see if the team behind it has experience in running a seven- or eight-figure business and that it's not just four 20-year-olds who have created a crypto from their bedroom and never run a business before.

Mistake 15: Mobile phone trading

> Trading on your mobile phone will burn a hole through your pocket faster than a set of keys for a new car.

I can confidently attribute at least £26,000 worth of my losing trades in my first year to trading on my mobile. I vividly remember one day when I was on a train to London and reading what I thought at the time was a really good trading email update. For some reason I believed every word this 'guru' was saying and how the euro was about to fall against the dollar. Being the naive newbie that I was, I looked at the chart, it looked all right-ish, so I blindly followed him into this trade and sold the equivalent amount of about 1 million euros. I opened up my trading app, punched in the relevant details and watched my money run away like a wild horse. It was as though the whole market was waiting for me to enter, then as soon as I did, it rallied with a big spike up after spike up after spike up.

Within minutes I was about £6,000 down. I should have killed the position instantly but, like most beginners, I fell into the trap of relying on hope, wishing it would come back. Instead of cutting my losers short and letting my winners run, I let my loser run ... and run and run ... until I blew about £10,000 with that single trade!

Upon further investigation I realized that, if I had had my laptop and looked at the chart properly, I would never have entered it. The picture the chart was showing was awful, but as my mobile phone's screen size was small the chart wasn't showing me the full picture.

Siam's tips

- **Always enter your trades from a laptop or computer.** Never use your mobile for this.
- **Do use your phone to monitor trades.** Closing losing positions or locking in profits with your stop losses is OK to do on your phone but just use it as a monitoring device, not a platform for analysis or placing trades.

Mistake 16: Snatching at profits

> Without doubt the hardest thing *not* to do ...

Snatching at profits is something you are bound to do. No matter how blunt I have been in this and the previous chapter, you will at some point ignore or forget my stark and detailed warnings. It's just human nature. You need to let your winners run and cut your losers short. This all stems back to sound risk management and risk-to-reward ratios, but you really, *really* do need to let your winners run. It's these runners that will completely offset all your losing trades, and then some. I tend to make about 3–15 per cent per month (around 3–7 per cent on average) but every now and then, because I'm a trend trader, I will latch on to a trend and ride it to its full extent. Sometimes a single trade will return me 10 per cent or more. Also, at least once a year I get into a trade that will make me 30 per cent plus. That's why you need to let your winners run.

However, I can fully understand how hard it is to resist the urge to snatch. Whether you close the trade to realize the profits or move your stop loss right up close to the market price in order to lock in as much profit as you can, just resist. For instance, if you're in a trade that is now £5,000 in profit, every single bone in your body will be screaming at you to lock in, say, £4,000, or even £3,000. Resist! You need to completely ignore the monetary value of the trade and place your stop loss according to the teachings you have learned.

I still struggle with this sometimes. It wasn't long ago that I was in a trade that was about £12,400 in profit. It was a beautiful US dollar/Chinese yuan trade and I was shorting it (essentially betting that the US dollar would go down). It was a really nice downward trend I was riding, then very quickly my profits jumped from about £8,000 to £12,400 (there was a spike down). My whole body was yelling at me to lock in the profits, but I just had to resist and leave my stop loss where it was. The probability of it rebounding back was high, so I stayed put. A few days later it rebounded back and then kept on falling. If I had snatched, I would have missed out on the subsequent continuation of the trend.

Siam's tips

- Stick to your training on where and how you move your stop losses.
- Try your hardest not to snatch.
- Make sure you're not snatching at a profit that is below your 1:2 risk-to-reward ratio. In other words, if you are going to snatch, keep your profits, at a minimum, above twice that of your expected risk on that trade.
- Once you place your trade, stick to your training. Get rid of the screen that shows you how much money you're up or down. Just look at the chart.

Mistake 17: Taking advice from poor people

> Would you ever take dieting advice from an obese
> binge eater?

Taking investment advice from poor people is an interesting topic because everyone does it. The other day I thought I'd have a look back over my trading/investing history. I was amazed at some of the risks and dodgy trades I placed in my first year, but the curious thing that stood out the most in my diary was the red star I'd marked next to every time I'd taken someone's advice *not* to do something. I call it my 'missed opportunity star' and it illustrates a very important point: who we take or don't take advice from is crucial to our finances.

Would you take fitness advice from a 20-stone binge eater? You wouldn't, so why on earth would you take financial advice from someone who's financially illiterate – or investment advice from someone who doesn't invest with their own money? I have a strict rule that I only take business advice from successful business owners, investment advice from successful investors and general pensions/wills/trusts advice from IFAs.

I saw that most of my red stars were from occasions where I'd listened to either a friend or an IFA to not invest in something, only to find out that their advice was grossly wrong and I'd missed out on a winner. Statistics show that a huge majority of IFAs, accountants or solicitors don't invest with their own money and they nearly all earn a living just from their nine-to-five wages rather than from returns on their investments. That's why I *never* take investment advice from people in these professions.

Siam's tips

- **Take advice only from successful investors of their own money.** Next time a friend, parent, stockbroker, journalist or anyone else tells you that a stock/commodity/investment product is a winner/loser, just do a double-check to see how that person makes their money.
- **Develop a keen sense of discernment or a BS detector.** This should help to keep you out of trouble.
- **If you insist on jumping into something on a 'tip', at least risk very little of your total capital.**

Mistake 18: Ignoring research bias

You need to discard your pride in investing and trading. Don't feel as though you always have to be correct in your market opinions, otherwise you'll fool yourself into making costly decisions.

Back when I was 19 and starting to 'dabble' with penny shares (yes, we've all been there), I remember a share tip from a friend. He said I really needed to buy Desire Petroleum shares. Being new to all of this and trusting him, as he seemed knowledgeable, I bought some DES shares with minimal research. After a month, my shares were up by about 10 per cent – I thought I was Gordon Gekko! So I bought more … and more. I became a little obsessed with this company and was reading all sorts of things about them on trading forums, trading websites and journals. It got to the stage where I was actually quite delusional about DES and thought that this share could only go one way: up.

The more I research I did, the more I found to contradict my 'bullish' opinions. But I dismissed it all. I remember being so biased towards DES that I discarded an important bit of information about the company's debt. If I had looked at this bit of evidence with a clear head, I would have immediately exited from that stock. But I didn't. I saw only what I wanted to see. As a result, I lost over £1,500 – a big loss for me at the time.

Siam's tips

- **With investing, be like a Vulcan and use logic and reason above all else.** The big lesson I learned here is that one should be systematic, have no emotions or attachments to your investment, and know that there may be a huge piece of the puzzle you're missing. Now, before I even consider any investment, all I do is actively search for reasons *not* to invest. Believe it or not, even now I still actively investigate why I should *not* invest in silver and gold. I'm still looking …

- **Be totally flexible with trading and investing.** Just because you thought or said an asset was going to go up, the moment you realize you were wrong, you need to either exit your position or reverse it. Notable billionaires like George Soros have been completely wrong on the news several times now, but they are always the first to admit their error and will react accordingly.

Mistake 19: Using too many indicators

> If your chart looks like spaghetti, you are likely to fail.

When new traders start out, they eventually read up on indicators. Just as I said there are thousands of trading strategies, there are also thousands of different chart indicators: Bollinger Bands, Stochastics, MACD, Fibonacci, Parabolic SAR and ·Moving Averages, to name a few.

Ultimately, every indicator is just a bunch of squiggly lines reporting all sorts of information, like whether the market is overbought or sold, whether the market is trending and so on. The common pitfall here is to load up your chart with lots of different indicators, but more than three is too much. It results in a very messy screen and you'll be obscuring what the market is actually doing.

When you're looking at the charts, all you should really care about is price action:

- What has the price done?
- What is the price doing now?
- In light of the patterns that form from the lows, highs and movements of the price, what is the price likely to do in the future?

That's all you should care about. Indicators can be a big distraction if you're not careful, so don't let them overwhelm you!

Siam's tip

- **If you have a good trading strategy, you should have no more than three indicators.**

- **If you don't have a specific strategy, still try not to have too many indicators.** If you do, you'll suffer from analysis paralysis. Some indicators will contradict others and you'll end up not placing trades or placing bad ones.

Mistake 20: No detailed trading plan or log

> Building a house without following a plan may result in wasted time and money. The same principle applies to trading.

Whenever Ellie (my lovely wife) and I have dinner in front of the TV, the programme *Grand Designs* always seems to be on. So we watch it and I'm amazed to see how many homeowners blindly jump into their huge property reconstruction without any blueprints, plans or advice from architects. They just do it on a whim and nearly every episode ends with the homeowners overspending by a large amount and the project taking longer than anticipated. This same haphazard approach happens with trading. I was a prime example when I started out. You really do need to have a detailed plan before you start.

I've met many traders in my time – many good ones and even more bad ones. The good ones are hard to find, as successful traders tend to be isolated and low key. They trade because they love it and they don't have much of an ego. In the very good book by Jack Schwager, *Market Wizards: Interviews with Top Traders*, there's a chapter where a trader called Brian Gelber talks about the big 1987 market crash and how the newspapers identified an alleged supertrader who made $20 million from the crash in just two weeks. This 'supertrader' had huge press coverage for weeks and he seemed to love it. Meanwhile, Brian quietly made around $20 million in 20 minutes at the same time but he's completely unknown. And Brian is very strict about using his journal.

> What I've found is that the single tool or habit that differentiates good traders from the rest is the adherence to a strict trading plan and trading journal.

Most retail traders (private traders like you and me) fail in this area because they treat it either like a lottery or casino or as a hobby. If you treat trading as a hobby, you'll get hobby-like results. You really do need to treat this as a business, and two of the main ways you can do that are by trading within the parameters of a strict trading plan (so this forces you to just take the low-hanging fruit) and by keeping an accurate log or journal of your activity/results. For most people, this is too much of a 'chore' and they eventually give up.

Siam's tips

- **Trade only in accordance with your trading plan.** Treat this like a business and be disciplined.
- **Maintain a journal or log of all the trades you place.** You can use pen and paper or keep an electronic spreadsheet. Track all your profits, losses, entries, exits, maximum risk and reasons why you entered/exited the trades. My students and I use our own developed journaling software where everyone's journal is open for everyone else to see, so you can have a look at everyone else's trades (including mine). Whenever you place a trade, you log it with this software and take an entry and exit screenshot. I print out these trades with their

screenshots and put them all into a folder for reviewing. Over time this becomes a treasure chest of information and analytical data. You'll be able to identify all sorts of trends or habits that lose you money. This is the best way to maintain a log, despite the paper and ink costs.

Mistake 21: Poor personal data security

> You are your biggest online threat!

Cryptos have a weird and wonderful way of taking you from a place of zero knowledge about IT security to one of being incredibly proficient at it – and all because you're now managing and securing your own money. Personal monetary sovereignty isn't all fun and games when you're looking after a six-, seven- or eight-figure portfolio.

And even though there have been many prolific hackings (and even physical hijackings), these attacks will most likely be picking off targets of high value – not the average crypto punter but high-profile crypto YouTubers, hedge fund managers and crypto founders. Nine times out of ten, if you lose any of your funds, it will be all your own fault, either because you have sloppy security habits or because you've mistyped an address.

Siam's tips

- **Create strong passwords and have a different password for everything.** Make your email password the hardest and most secure because most password resets are done via email. Get your emails hacked and you're a goner.

- **Don't keep any passwords on a cloud storage service.** This includes Google Keep, Dropbox, Google Drive and Evernote. You literally don't own the information you upload, the entity does. Plus, they're easy to hack.
- **Get rid of all default settings with your modem or Internet hub.** I was astounded when a BT call handler once logged into my router from halfway around the world and started fiddling with it. You have to close that back door.
- *Never* **use public Wi-Fi services on the computer you use for your crypto activity.** And don't use the computer that you use to visit dodgy websites.
- **Always back up your data.** Make three different copies with two different media, with at least one kept offsite.
- *Always* **double-check the addresses you're sending your cryptos to before hitting the submit button.** You may not have correctly copied and pasted the address.
- **It's worth getting a non-data-logging VPN.** If you are forced to use a public Wi-Fi, this means that you can access it via your VPN. I personally use Express VPN as it's fast for streaming Netflix if I'm ever abroad.

25
What will the world of crypto look like in 20 years?

'Forecast what may happen but don't put a darn date on it.'

Unknown

It won't be long before you start seeing articles all over the Internet trying to gauge what the future is going to look like for cryptos.

The next one to five years can sometimes be accurately forecast, as the markets are very much like large weather systems. If you saw a large hurricane slowly tracking up towards Florida, you could extrapolate the speed and track of the hurricane to work out semi-accurately the time when Florida would be hit. You could then place investments based on this, like buying orange juice futures in anticipation of the orange groves being decimated, or buying shares in the companies that the government will contract for rebuilding the infrastructure.

Reading the future any further than that is hard, especially long-term (20-year) forecasts, as there are so many variables. Nevertheless, I'm going to give it my best shot and you can all buy me a beer in 20 years if I'm right. I'm going to approach this methodically, starting with a view from 30,000 feet and working our way down into the weeds.

The view from 30,000 feet: network ruler cryptonomics

You may remember my all-important mantra I cited at the beginning of this book: cryptos are the evolution of money and blockchain is the revolution of trust. The first bit of that is quite straightforward, as it doesn't take much imagination to see how conventional money and the banking sector are going to be dramatically disrupted over the next 20 years. But the 'revolution of trust' bit ... what does it really mean?

In essence, it means that anything that requires or controls trust will be disintermediated. That is the crypto/DLT superpower. Just as the Incredible Hulk will smash things and Thor will fling his hammer about, the crypto superpower is the streamlining of inefficient businesses and industries and the disintermediation of power and control over networks. The net result or residue from this superpower is that networks will be replaced by markets.

Think about this for a second. **Markets will replace networks.**

It's a weird concept to grasp but it's a bit like how the Internet had the effect of replacing monopolies with competition. Before the Internet, most communication was handled by large state entities like British Telecom. With the advent of the Internet and deregulation, communication became faster and cheaper, sparking a competition war and reducing prices, which was great for end users.

The power landscape

To fully understand how markets will replace networks, you need to understand the power landscape.

Humans are the prime networked species on Earth. Since the development of language, maybe even before then, we have networked. We are forever creating bridges that connect our networks – bridges like tin cans with strings, fax, SMS, roads, airways and the Internet – all so that we can communicate with our tribes and communities. But what history has shown us is that we don't do well in leaderless communities and so leaders emerge. We've had kings, lords, emperors and presidents controlling the big networks for thousands of years.

Historically, nations are the main networks these leaders have ruled, but the Industrial Revolution sparked a new world necessity for energy and money. These new networks quickly became the most important to own and control. Every country on the planet is a slave to energy and money, which are now the top-level, Level 1 networks.

There have always been conflicts between Level 2 networks such as governments and national leaders, who bicker among themselves, but in reality these leaders are one step down from the energy and money networks. Energy and money networks pull the strings because countries are completely reliant on them. A prime example of this is the famous Mayer Amschel Rothschild maxim from the late 1700s: 'Permit us control of the money of a country and we care not who makes its laws.'

> It's important to understand that the people with
> real power in the world are those who control
> globally scaled networks.

It's not a case of who is the most powerful among leaders such as Trump, Putin and Jinping. It's a question of who owns the networks that Trump, Putin and Jinping need. This inevitably leads to the conclusion that real power rests with whoever controls the global money network or the global energy network. This is why the likes of the Rothschilds, the Rockefellers and the owners of the Bank of International Settlements, the International Monetary Fund and the World Bank are the real puppeteers. Note that they are non-governmental entities with private shareholders.

The energy network explains why the West is meddling in Syria and will soon meddle in Iran. It's all to do with strategic positioning, energy reserves and, more importantly, the gas lines that should eventually succeed in providing Europe with natural gas.

Moving forward, conflicts and intrigue will escalate over the next 20 years in North Korea, which is sitting on $10 trillion worth of untapped mineral reserves. There's a good reason why the West doesn't invade countries like Zimbabwe or other countries with genocidal leaders: they have no resources. In the big picture, war is an investment activity. There *has* to be an ROI, which could be about money or take another form like positioning. The only way for North Korea to avoid the fate of Iraq, Afghanistan and Libya is to open up its borders and embrace the world.

Since the Industrial Revolution, Level 1 networks haven't faltered despite the pack of cards constantly shuffling beneath them. As well as energy and money, there are many more networks battling for power below them.

Religion is a network. A corporation is a network. Roads are a network. Electricity is a network. So, too, are telecommunications, pharmaceuticals, stock markets, weapons and intelligence. These are the Level 2 networks, and it's probably fair to assume that those who own or control the Level 1 networks also have influence over or own elements of the Level 2 networks.

As the Internet has matured over the last decade, we are seeing a new type of network appear. These are new Level 2 online networks like Facebook and Google, which are beginning to gain as much influence and power as some countries. Facebook has 2.1 billion monthly active users, so you may as well call Facebook's CEO King Zuckerberg.

Mark Zuckerberg could elevate his network into the big league as he pretty much has everyone's data and has trained us all to check our Facebook page every day like sheep. Facebook could easily become the next World Bank, or the biggest insurance company on the planet, or the biggest eBay. It would be incredibly convenient for everyone. And it's DLT and cryptos that can actually make all of this happen.

I'm going all in on Facebook Coin when they inevitably launch it. There's a new and growing currency out there at the moment and it's attention. Everyone is fighting for it and Facebook is a master of day trading attention. So FB Coin would have instant value because it would make all Facebook advertisers buy ad space via FB Coin. They might even do an airdrop to every user, like a form of global quantitative easing, to get it all kick-started. Write a good post and you could earn FB Coin for every 'like' or 'share' you get, which you could then spend on advertising or in the Facebook marketplace conveniently placed in the centre of every mobile Facebook app.

But going back to the point, the power is in the network controllers. That's why cryptos and DLTs are more important to the world than the invention of the Internet. Put it this way, what's more important to you, emails or money? Exactly … it's money.

You'll remember that the crypto/DLT superpower is streamlining and disintermediation. So right now the high-powered Level 2 network controllers fear being disintermediated by cryptos. How will they mitigate the risk?

Cryptos will replace networks with marketplaces – hundreds if not thousands of mini-markets. These markets are public, tamper-resistant, transparent, efficient, without middlemen, merit-based and leaderless. For example, there are people who control the stock markets. Ignore the name, it's actually a network and right now Stacey Cunningham could close down the New York Stock Exchange if she wanted to. China could close down the London Mercantile Exchange because China owns the London Mercantile Exchange. All these types of network are centralized and cryptos will disrupt them by creating markets. So, instead of a centralized stock market, there will be dozens of decentralized local stock markets. It is the 'trust nuke': anything that can be disintermediated or streamlined will be. Nothing will stop this revolution happening over the next 20 years.

You may not agree with the rather alarming assessment outlined above, and that's fine, but all I ask is that you always ask yourself 'Who gains from this?' when you see things on the news. Follow the money and it will lead you to the answer.

The view from 20,000 feet: the future tech landscape

A good way to focus on the future tech landscape is to rewind 20 years and imagine you are in the middle of the original tech bubble when someone asks you, 'What is the future of the Internet?' Obviously, you know what's happened. It's made the world a smaller place, increased the velocity of communications, which in turn has increased the velocity of money, which is why global GDP has soared. And the Internet has revolutionized almost every industry and micro-niche on the planet, from entertainment to dating to scientific research to secretly stalking old school friends. In a nutshell, it's been fantastic! The good the Internet does massively outweighs the bad. And it will be the same for cryptos.

The UK Treasury recently released a 110-page report called *UK National Risk Assessment of Money Laundering and Terrorist Financing*. In this riveting piece of work researchers produced a magnificent table (Table 25.1). From this you can see that digital currencies (cryptos) are the least risky vehicle on this list for money laundering, whereas the banks are the worst.

Going back to the question 'What is the future of the Internet?' it's a hard question without the aid of hindsight but a prominent techie, Clifford Stoll, nailed it back in 1995, while also miserably failing at the same time:

Visionaries see a future of telecommuting workers, interactive libraries and multimedia classrooms. They speak of electronic town meetings and virtual communities. Commerce and business will shift from offices and malls to networks and modems. And the freedom of digital networks will make government more democratic. Baloney. Do our computer pundits lack all common sense?

Newsweek, 26 February 1995

Thematic area	Total vulnerabilities score	Total likelihood score	Structural risk	Structural risk level	Risk with mitigation grading	Overall risk level
Banks	34	6	211	High	158	High
Accountancy service providers	14	9	120	High	90	High
Legal service providers	17	7	112	High	84	High
Money service businesses	18	7	119	High	71	Medium
Trust or company service providers	11	6	64	Medium	64	Medium
Estate agents	11	7	77	Medium	58	Medium
High-value dealers	10	6	56	Low	42	Low
Retail betting (unregulated gambling)	10	5	48	Low	36	Low
Casinos (regulated gambling)	10	3	32	Low	24	Low
Cash	21	7	147	High	88	High
New payment methods (e-money)	10	6	60	Medium	45	Medium
Digital currencies	5	3	15	Low	11	Low

TABLE 25.1 National risk assessment on money laundering, UK.
Source: UK Treasury.

Stoll was scarily accurate but he just couldn't believe it would happen. So next time you hear a vision for the future, don't be too quick to shoot it down. We are in the hockey stick part of exponential growth, and the future may in fact be far more advanced than you imagine, especially if what Google's Director of Engineering, Ray Kurzweil, says comes true. He talks about the 'singularity', where artificial intelligence becomes smarter than the human race. If this happened, AI would be able to create things that we literally can't comprehend.

Exponential growth

Another reason why trying to forecast the future is hard is because of exponential growth. This is something the human brain just can't compute unless you actively study its behaviour. We are hardwired to think in linear terms and so when something goes 1, 2, 3, 4, 5, 20, 1,000, 100,000, 100,000,000,000,000,000, it just smacks us in the face. This is why the next 20 years are going to be so incredibly different compared to the last 20 years.

A good way to get your head around this is to imagine that I took you to a large football or baseball stadium with a capacity of 90,000 people. Now let's say I handcuffed you to the very top row of seats and made the stadium watertight then skipped to the centre of the pitch and pulled out my pipette of magic water. The water is magic because when I drop it, it doubles in size every 60 seconds. So after one minute there are two drops. After two minutes there are four drops, and so on. Let's say I released one drop of this water on to the pitch at midday.

What time do you think the stadium would fill up? Most people are way out. The answer is that you'll be screaming for your life at 12.50, just 50 minutes later. And here's the bizarre thing about exponential growth. At 12.45, just five minutes before the stadium overflows, the stadium will still be 97 per cent empty. That's the thing that catches humans out all the time! We think nothing is wrong, and then – BAM.

Exponential growth creates a progress deception chart like this:

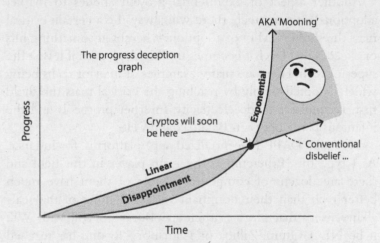

FIGURE 25.2 The progress deception graph

A prime example of how a conventional industry is going to be overhauled and deceived by linear thinking is the VISA network. The rate of growth VISA has made is pretty much linear as it's scaled up in line with demand, to the point where right now it does about 24,000 transactions per second. Cryptos have struggled to get anywhere near this but we are rapidly nearing the linear/exponential crossover point. We may even have already overtaken the linear line now that there are cryptos like Nano with instant transactions, zero fees and unlimited scalability. This is something VISA can't compete with and, by the time a conventional/linear entity or organization wakes up, if the exponential tech is anywhere near the crossover blob, it's far too late. By the time VISA can scale up to handle, say, 1 million transactions per second (TPS), the average crypto will no doubt easily handle hundreds of millions of transactions per second.

Another aspect of exponential growth applies to market adoption. With any tech, there will always be a certain critical mass threshold (CMT) of adoption, whereby if something hits or exceeds that level, it becomes the 'big dog', even if it isn't the superior tech. There are many examples of inferior techs being widely adopted simply by reaching the critical mass threshold first. Examples include electricity, Internet protocols and the infamous battle between Betamax and VHS.

Let's take DAPP (decentralized app) platforms, for instance. As I type this, Ethereum is the main player in this field and there are dozens of competitors. Most of them have much better tech than their dominant rival and none of the scalability issues that plague Ethereum. But who will win? Will it be NEO, Qtum, Zilliqa or Cardano? No one has reached that critical mass threshold yet. But Ethereum is ahead of the pack because it was around first and it has had a nice boost from being the go-to platform for ICOs. Despite Ethereum's issues, if it hits the CMT first, it's pretty much game over for the runners-up (see Figure 25.2). This is because, by the time a runner-up hits the CMT, Ethereum will be long gone and way up that vertical line. It's much like the way WordPress is the main website building platform, even though there are hundreds of better alternatives.

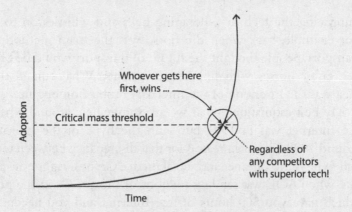

FIGURE 25.2 Whoever hits the CMT first wins

Where will we be with cryptos?

What will the world look like in 20 years' time? If it's a barren wasteland, then cryptos won't exist. But if it's anything like most sci-fi films, then cryptos will be the cornerstone of that world. Personally, I think it will be a mix of both. The rich/poor divide is not a social problem, it's a mathematical certainty. If you have debt, compounding interest works against you. If you have capital, compounding interest boosts you. So the current divide can only increase.

In addition, the tech we have today has been created with current thinking to solve current problems. And the problems of the future will require new thinking and new tech. In all probability, this will take the form of tech and problems we can't even dream of right now.

Where most people go wrong with forecasting technological development is that they take an existing tech and project it forwards using linear thinking. This is the equivalent of improving the tech by sellotaping bells and whistles on to it. For example, back when the horse was the main method of transport, people thought the future of transport would be bigger, faster horses with improved carriages. What ruined this idea was the invention of the internal combustion engine.

My best estimation is that we are somewhere around where the Internet was in 1994 but with the hype of the Internet around 1998. The main reason for that discrepancy between tech and hype is the Internet and social media. Cryptos right now are like when AOL was sending millions of those CDs in the post which gave you 500 hours of free Internet and you needed a modem the size of a house to connect.

Even though we have some mighty cryptos out there, with tens of billions of dollars of market cap like Bitcoin, Ether, Litecoin and so on, I genuinely believe these are the equivalent of AOL, Netscape and Altavista. This means that cryptos now are akin to VHS; we know they're here to stay but they're not the future. Just as VHS was succeeded first by DVD and then by Netflix, so, too, will cryptos be succeeded by something else.

As the progress deception graph shows, when it comes to the tech side, we are well and truly in the Dip of Disappointment where we are still hampered by Generation 1 and 2 distributed ledger technologies (DLTs), with transaction fees, speed and scalability issues, choke points and network leaders – even though Generation 3 DLTs exist. In the future, the thought of waiting up to two hours for a bank transfer to complete or not being able to do banking on a weekend will seem utterly archaic. So, too, will the concept of paying for transaction fees or having to wait for transactions to go through.

I have the utmost respect for Bitcoin inventor Satoshi Nakamoto, whose identity remains a mystery, but Satoshi didn't know everything. Satoshi probably didn't anticipate the crypto's rate of adoption, or how this new ecosystem would develop and in what direction. For instance, Bitcoin was created to be a global currency but it's now far from that as it's turned into a speculative investment that no one wants to transact with. This is why the whole debate about Bitcoin Core versus Bitcoin Cash is such a waste of time. If Bitcoin were even to match the scale of VISA with 24 k TPS, it would need a block size of about 400 terabytes! This is why Generation 1 and 2 DLTs are having to resort to off-chain scaling solutions like the Lightning Network for Bitcoin, Raiden for Ethereum and Plasma for Omisego. These off-chain solutions are the equivalent of a Sellotape bodge-job as they actually make decentralized networks more centralized, which isn't good due to concentration risk. This picture illustrates the point:

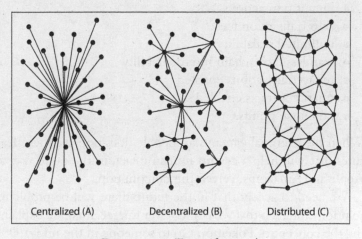

FIGURE 25.3 Types of network

A: This is a centralized network. It's what most networks on the planet look like. If you wanted to take out the network, you'd target the central node.

B: This is what a decentralized network would look like with an off-chain scaling solution such as the Lightning Network. An example of an off-chain solution would be you setting up a float between you and a friend. You both put £100 into a pot and then, whenever you and your friend transact, deal or borrow from each other, you simply keep a tab according to the float. This way, all those hundreds or thousands of transactions don't need to be computed on the main network. This 'tab' is only computed on the main network once it is settled, closed or increased. Thus it creates lots of centralized nodes.

C: This is what a properly distributed network should look like. There are no leaders and no choke points.

I believe the absolute **minimum benchmark standard for DLTs** in the future should be:

- instant transactions
- zero transaction fees
- unlimited scalability
- seamless cross-chain interoperability
- micro transactions enabled
- smart contracts enabled
- no choke points.

When the eventual gargantuan bubble does pop, it's these features that will help a crypto remain intact, in the same way as Apple and Amazon survived the dotcom pop.

We need to accept that in the future there will be problems, solutions and tech that we could never foresee. Imagine explaining the concept of Pokémon Go to someone in the mid-1990s. It would have been laughable, but 20 years later Pokémon Go amassed 65 million users within nine months of launching.

I consider myself a realistic optimist and, although I see tremendous economic and geopolitical upheaval happening over

the next ten years, I do believe that as a species we can overcome dilemmas with tech and resourcefulness. After all the desperate power and land grabs, I believe we will live in a world of
abundance that cryptos will help positively shape.

We are in an amazing position now, where multiple techs
are about to hit the 'hockey stick growth curve' of exponential
growth. In the 1990s we had just one: the Internet. Now we have:

- bio-nano tech
- AI
- 3D printing
- robotics
- drones
- IoT
- VR/AR
- cryptos
- wireless data projection
- supermaterials.

So our 'hockey stick growth curve' looks something like this:

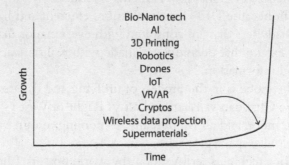

FIGURE 25.4 The 'hockey stick growth curve' of various new
technologies

The Internet, which is just one single tech, has spurned thousands, if not millions, of different techs and use cases. Just as the Internet has mated RFID chips, which spawned the off-spring tech of contactless debit cards, we will see an endless number of amazing permutations when all these techs take off.

We could have wireless VR contact lenses that would enable us to go and gamble in Las Vegas, with our wins and losses connected to our real-life crypto wallets. AI-controlled drones could be connected to an emergency services blockchain and automatically deliver a do-it-yourself defibrillator or a shot of bio-nano tech medicine if you're having a heart attack. Houses might be 3D printed for under £10 k and physically installed by robots in a fraction of the time it takes today. The scope is limitless.

I would like to believe that in the future our children and grandchildren will live in an abundant world where they enjoy the following benefits:

- The political voting system is open, online, trustworthy and tamper-resistant.
- The size of global governments is reduced by 90 per cent because DLTs are much more efficient and have AI advisers that are consulted with every major matter, to ensure that decisions are made with real statistics and information.
- The globe is in the process of unifying and debates like Christian vs Islam or Left vs Right or West vs East are moot; and all we humans are pooling resources to colonize space properly.
- Space tech gets serious focus by world powers. I have great admiration for Elon Musk and have every faith that he will deliver on all his goals, which will help us all no end.

- Universal Basic Income (UBI) is in place, as 3D printing, AI and robotics have consumed 90 per cent of jobs. UBI would enable humans to be free to do whatever we want. In essence, we embrace the AI job-stealing tsunami and up-level everyone. (It's just like how today 90 per cent of the population doesn't have to work the land any more. We outsourced that job to machinery.)
- Business will have AI advisers and robots to carry out menial work, so employees of the future will be doing much higher-level activities. This will lead to a big gig economy where the average person will be more of a one-man band/freelancer.
- Energy is abundant and freely distributed.
- Communication is free, instant, unlimited, uncensored and distributed.
- Transport is free and fast and road fatalities are a barbaric historical statistic.
- People go off grid in many forms from energy, water and food.
- VR becomes indistinguishable from reality for all our senses. The possibilities here are limitless. Watch the film *Ready Player One* for a glimpse of what VR could be like. It's shocking, chilling and amazing all at the same time.

The view from 10,000 feet: possible use cases

We're making progress! We're now down to the last stage of our forecast where we jump into the weeds and imagine a potential future day. Some of the following suggestions may seem to have nothing to do with cryptos or DLTs but they will be a fundamental part of these ideas, in the same way as pretty much every tech needs the Internet at some point. Here goes:

1 You wake up fully refreshed. A bad night of sleep is a thing of the past.

2 Every room has smart lights and smart heating, all controlled by a central, private, secure home–AI that knows you and your habits. The lights turn on in anticipation of you walking to the bathroom, and the hallways and rooms you normally use are perfectly heated. There's no energy wastage as a result. And you don't feel guilty because your home energy is clean and abundant. In fact, your home contributes to the national grid because you're generating excess energy from your Tesla roof, solar windows and battery packs. The National Grid kickbacks you get are real time and you are paid instantly via crypto into your wallet per joule of energy you create. There are also smart contracts, which automatically send a percentage of your earned energy money to a charity. So you're automatically donating to charity with money you've generated for free. It's all on autopilot. Sweet!

3 You have a shower, using fully recycled and cleaned water that is not from a water company.

4 You brush your teeth, using your smart toothbrush. It analyses your spit and sends the information down to your kitchen 3D printer. This 3D printer will make your favourite cup of coffee and also a breakfast bar filled with all the nutrients you are lacking. This will prevent 90 per cent of all ailments and diseases, which will save the health sector billions per year.

5 You no longer have to do any shopping. Your 3D printer makes your food and everything else you need.

Amazon will no doubt have pivoted to being the main place to go to download the 3D schematics for your 3D printer if you want a new toy or other item, or for your 3D printing refills, which are automatically ordered and installed for you.

6 You go to work – except that it's not really work. You receive a UBI, which frees you up from employment, so you're just working on your own new business project with AI/robotic assistants. You're running this business for fun, not because you have to pay your mortgage.

7 When you need new equipment, such as a new expensive 3D printer, raising the finance to acquire it is simple. It will take just hours to raise the capital because thousands of people in your local area who will use your business will donate a small amount directly to your crypto wallet. They will then get an ROI because, for every widget your new machine makes that you sell, your funders will automatically and instantly get a cut of the profits until everyone gets their ROI and your machine is fully paid off. Beautiful! One of the barriers to fundraising has been that funders may not trust or understand where their investment capital will go. This way there is no concern that it will be wasted. As such, there are now also thousands of local stock markets around the world like a Norwich or Manchester stock market. This means that if you want to invest in the future of a particular local business, you can.

8 Money itself as we know it will be entirely alien to us. After nations around the world 'cryptofy' their sovereign currencies, there will be a logical and persistent shift towards two global currencies: the global spending coin and the global saver coin. The reason that Bitcoin

became a speculative asset is because it had inbuilt scarcity and so no one wanted to spend it because the price of it just kept increasing. It became the first global saving coin due to its deflationary effects. And you use the official Global Reserve currency, which may be the IMF SDR, as your spending coin, as it's what you need to pay your taxes and it's inflationary because there is likely to be no cap on how many SDRs can exist.

9 It's time to go home. Your automated Tesla comes to pick you up. Your ownership of this Tesla is effectively free, because for the 90 per cent of the day where you don't need it, it functions as a minicab earning money for you. And it earns enough so that your monthly finance for the car is covered. It even plugs itself in and recharges when it needs to. As driving is all automated and no one dies on the road any more, car insurance costs have dropped 90 per cent. There aren't any deaths because every automated car is on a blockchain with central AI oversight. There are also no traffic lights and far fewer cars on the road, and journeys are 50 per cent faster.

10 You're now home from work and want to do something fun with the kids, so you all go skydiving over the islands of Hawaii in VR. It's just as good as the real thing as the VR goggles or contact lenses have the same, if not better, resolution than human eyesight.

11 You fancy a quick weekend getaway with the family, so you simply jump on to a Space X rocket taxi and fly from the UK to Sydney in under an hour, all for the price of a normal airline ticket ...

... I could go on all day.

In terms of cryptos, I believe we will have our main two spending and saving cryptos and then a plethora of other cryptos. Remember, you can't really have a blockchain or DLT without a token. Otherwise it's like having a stock market without any stocks. So there will be a sea of cryptos/DLTs all being extremely good in their own particular niches. But cross-chain integration is effortless, just like an ecommerce website that normally integrates with PayPal in a few clicks.

We've skimmed through the iceberg-sized topics of network ruler cryptonomics, the possible future landscape and some possible everyday use cases. Will this all happen within 20 years? Maybe, maybe not. Some ideas may take 50 years. But I hope it's enough information to really get you thinking.

Final thoughts

> Just focus on what you can control and do it!

Despite this *Star Trek*-like utopia I've illustrated, I don't think we will ever truly eliminate and disintermediate the real network rulers of the world – whoever they are. They will just pivot and continue secretly to pull the strings. It's just human nature, after all. If a group of power-hungry individuals own and control the world, they also have the means and motive to ensure that their grip remains, whether that grip is overt or covert. Since this is all out of our control, I wouldn't mull over it too much.

However, there's an interesting question I like asking in crypto groups, as it always sparks some riveting conversation. And that question is: 'Who created Bitcoin? Was it a lonely individual or was it the elites?'

I love hearing people's views on this question, as the range of answers and thoughts is fascinating. I sat on the fence on this topic for a fair while, as my views are controversial enough, but the more I learn and the more I live the crypto life, the more I am leaning towards the elites. The reason for this is that history shows us numerous occasions in many different cultures where the elites go to great lengths to retain their control whenever their grip starts loosening. As time goes by and the masses become savvier, these measures become more extreme.

For instance, in the early 1900s the US Stock Market tumbled and this was followed by the panic of 1907, after which the public developed a deep resentment of central bankers. It was even written in the US Constitution that private entities should not control the US money supply. What happened? In 1910 a small group of central bankers, politicians and financiers secretly met on Jekyll Island in the USA to come up with a plan for a new banking system and central bank. Some of these founders were big names such as the Warburgs and the Rockefellers. They travelled alone, at night, without an entourage and used only their first names. Because these people were well known at the time, if the public saw that they were meeting in secret it would have raised suspicion. After all, it was as though the foxes were meeting to discuss the building and security system of a new chicken shed.

Long story short, after three years they finally got the Federal Reserve approved and the USA once again had a private entity as a central bank controlling the US money supply, with private shareholders earning 6 per cent in dividends per year. I would strongly encourage you to read G. Edward Griffin's book *The Creature from Jekyll Island* or watch the video about it on You-Tube, both of which explain it beautifully.

Going back to the original question, what inspired it was a front cover of *The Economist* from September 1988, which had the headline 'Get Ready for a World Currency by 2018'. It predicted the end of paper money and the introduction of a new global currency. This new money seems eerily similar to Bitcoin and there was talk of how the 'elites' want a one-world government and one-world money. And there is also this quote from the founder of Ford which has stuck in my mind:

> It is well enough that people of the nation do not understand our banking and monetary system, for if they did, I believe there would be a revolution before tomorrow morning.

About 12 years before Bitcoin was created, the National Security Agency effectively created the blueprint of cryptocurrencies and Bitcoin's foundation when NSA cryptographers published a paper called 'How to Make a Mint: The Cryptography of Anonymous Electronic Cash' and circulated it around MIT and the *American Law Review*. The paper outlined everything Bitcoin, all the way down to the security protocol that is used to secure Bitcoin – SHA-256-bit encryption. Again, the NSA created SHA-256 encryption.

Everything I've mentioned so far is fact. This is where I jump off the ship and whether you follow me is up to you. We now know that the US Government or the elites that control it had the capability and resources to create Bitcoin. It would also have seen that the US dollar was in a terminal decline and that eventually the public would grow to hate Wall Street and the banking system just as the US public did in 1907. I believe they had the motive to make Bitcoin, as it's the only way they could continue to control their various networks.

Think about it. The people who oppose a one-world government and world money are a large demographic consisting of extremists, the anti-establishment and libertarians. These people would fight tooth and nail against something like that. And, like a textbook manoeuvre from Sun Tzu's *Art of War*, I believe that the elites *used* this very demographic to embrace and propagate this new world money. They created Bitcoin as a Trojan-horse currency that would revolutionize money and banking and give power back to the people … and the world lapped it up.

Here we are now, privileged to be witnessing an evolution of money in the making, with front-row seats to what could possibly be the greatest public hoodwink in history. It seems to explain why there is so much secrecy around Satoshi. And where are the 1 million Bitcoin that Satoshi mined that have never been moved?

You may think this a pretty outlandish theory with which to end this book. But whether you agree or disagree with it, don't let it get in the way of the teachings and information in this guide. If you do agree and you're appalled by it all, don't let it prevent you from making profits in this market. In fact, make it your mission to profit as much as you can so that you can enhance your life and those around you and then do good in the world. No matter how small or big that good may be, just do it.

Taking it further

I hope this book will be a bit of a crypto bible for you to refer to now and then, but if you want to take your crypto investing to the next level, I'd highly recommend you join our fabulous crypto community over at www.TheRealisticTrader.com. We have the most active Facebook group I've ever seen, where all questions are answered within minutes; we hold a big 300–500-people event every three months with amazing guest speakers and more crypto content; and we hold a smaller 50–100-people gathering every two months with drinks, pizza and more crypto chat/debates and guest speakers. To top it off, when you join, you get free lifetime access to my Basic Crypto Investing Course for beginners and also a full one-day workshop with me and my team of crypto mentors that look after the community. It's a brilliant family to be a part of and I do hope to meet you one day in person.

So once again, thank you for taking the time to read this book. It's truly appreciated, and happy HODLing!

Index